New Technologies and the Media

Key Concerns in Media Studies

Series editor: Andrew Crisell

Within the context of today's global, digital environment, *Key Concerns in Media Studies* addresses themes and concepts that are integral to the study of media. Concisely written by leading academics, the books consider the historical development of these themes and the theories that underpin them, and assess their overall significance, using up-to-date examples and case studies throughout. By giving a clear overview of each topic, the series provides an ideal starting point for all students of modern media.

Published

Andrew Crisell   *Liveness and Recording in the Media*

Tim Dwyer   *Legal and Ethical Issues in the Media*

Gerard Goggin   *New Technologies and the Media*

Shaun Moores   *Media, Place and Mobility*

Forthcoming

Paul Bowman   *Culture and the Media*

Bob Franklin   *Politics, News and the Media*

Gerard Goggin and Kathleen Ellis   *Disability and the Media*

David Hendy   *Public Service Broadcasting*

Niall Richardson and Sadie Wearing   *Gender and the Media*

New Technologies and the Media

First published 2012 by
PALGRAVE MACMILLAN

Palgrave Macmillan in the UK is an imprint of Macmillan Publishers Limited, registered in England, company number 785998, of Houndmills, Basingstoke, Hampshire RG21 6XS.

Palgrave Macmillan in the US is a division of St Martin's Press LLC, 175 Fifth Avenue, New York, NY 10010.

Palgrave Macmillan is the global academic imprint of the above companies and has companies and representatives throughout the world.

Palgrave® and Macmillan® are registered trademarks in the United States, the United Kingdom, Europe and other countries

ISBN-13: 978–0–230–28221–6

This book is printed on paper suitable for recycling and made from fully managed and sustained forest sources. Logging, pulping and manufacturing processes are expected to conform to the environmental regulations of the country of origin.

A catalogue record for this book is available from the British Library.

A catalog record for this book is available from the Library of Congress.

10   9   8   7   6   5   4   3   2   1
21   20   19   18   17   16   15   14   13   12

Printed and bound in Great Britain by
CPI Antony Rowe, Chippenham and Eastbourne

For Bianca and Liam

Contents

Acknowledgements

In the writing of this book I have incurred many debts, only some of which I can enumerate here.

Many thanks to Andrew Crisell for approaching me to write the book in the first place, and for his warm support, acuity and gracious example through his own writings. I am grateful to my publisher Rebecca Barden, whom I was very pleased to encounter again, and the team at Palgrave Macmillan for their impeccable work.

I wish to thank colleagues in the Journalism and Media Research Centre, University of New South Wales for their support. In particular, I benefited greatly from many stimulating conversations about the future of newspapers and journalism with David McKnight, who also read a chapter of this book. I would like to record my gratitude to colleagues in the Department of Media and Communications, University of Sydney, where the book was finished – especially Penny O'Donnell for her comments. My long-time friend and collaborator Jock Given offered characteristically astute suggestions on television and new technology. I also benefited greatly from numerous conversations about the press with Greg Bearup, writer, journalist and my neighbour, interspersed with spates of community gardening and minding each other's children.

Finally, and foremost, the book was made possible, as always, by the love and support of my partner, Jacqueline, and children, Liam and Bianca. Jacqui, the veteran of many books, was unstinting in her encouragement and interest; Liam was kind enough to ask me sensitively and often how many pages I had left to write; and Bianca sparkled in all sorts of ways, especially as the littlest and most adroit iPadiste.

Gerard Goggin

1 Introduction

For the past three decades, new technologies have played an increasingly influential role in media. In the 2010s, the dynamics of media – its changes and reforms, its challenges and futures – are inextricably bound up with new technologies. For those who study and care about media, a critical understanding of new technologies is essential, as we encounter claims, assumptions, uses, visions, hype and reliance on new technologies wherever we turn to make sense of media.

In this light, *New Technologies and the Media* aims to critically and accessibly introduce the real and serious issues at stake in media as they relate to technology. How do we understand the new audiences forming around user-generated content? What part does technology play in shaping the future of news and journalism? How are broadcasters confronting the challenges technology poses? Who pays for culture, when intellectual property is now so central? What is the place of new user cultures and practices in press and broadcasting (blogging, social media and citizen journalism versus the norms, skills and training of the cadre of professional journalists)? Finally, what are the cultural politics of digital cultures and technologies, and what are the distinctive new concerns raised for the media?

New Technologies and the Media arises from a personal concern that the role of new technologies in media transformations is not being effectively discussed or addressed because of a polarization between two tendencies of thought. This book aims to provide such an introduction by offering a concise, integrated and comprehensive account that brings together both sides of this coin (cf. Fenton, 2010a).

To greatly simplify, one camp holds that new technologies are not only bringing the media into crisis – but that they also provide the solution. The future of journalism, according to the pro-technology camp, lies neither in prospects of public or private trust-funding, nor does broadcasting needed to be supported via state funding or special licensing arrangements. Rather the new dispensation lies in the promise of decentralized but large-scale user practices and systems – from blogging through open news to video-sharing sites – to radically overhaul and improve what we formerly knew as the media.

The other group holds that the press still plays a vitally important political and social role, notwithstanding the destruction of its advertising-supported business model by the role of internet search engines. Moreover, defenders of traditional media cleave to the view that television and radio remain the tried, tested and still preferred media of national, international and local audiences. While broadcasting might be undergoing great changes, advocates point to the surprising resilience in the old order's adaptation of new formats, technologies and platforms. Adherents of this position scorn the much vaunted novelty of new technologies, question their actual usage and significance, doubting whether interactivity and users can really contribute in a high-quality and systematic way to media, or whether their economic contribution is, in fact, as valuable as claimed.

Of course, such a cartoon-like depiction of new vs old media when it comes to technologies is a patent generalization that neither does justice to the multiplicity of points of view on these debates, nor to the quality of the thinking that attaches to them. Unfortunately, my characterization does not lie too far from the mark. It is a matter of profound disappointment that much public discourse and debate about new technologies and the media, as well as research and teaching in media studies, does not come to grips with the pressing issues we currently face. Against this dichotomy of views, this book seeks to provide its readers with the concepts and tools to accurately analyse and evaluate new technologies – how they fit into and shape media. In doing so, it tries to plot a course through the clamour of actors, interests, promoters, resisters and sceptics that cluster around new technologies.

Media is one of the spheres of life most affected by new technologies. This is not only important for those who study, work in, care about or have an interest in media; it is important for everyone else too – because these very technologies are integrally involved in the developments that see media entrenched as a pervasive, intimate and powerful part of our lives. While there are many aspects of new technologies that touch media, this book focuses on print and broadcasting. Despite repeated and extravagant claims in the past two decades that both print and broadcasting are dead, they remain resilient. Their importance for society, culture, politics, economics and for both the private and public spheres not only endures, but has deepened as the media, through technology, has assumed new forms – the development, nature and significance of which are still not widely understood.

Broadly speaking, the book takes an *integrated media and cultural studies approach* to its topic. As I proceed, I try to recognize and explicate the role of various factors in the co-evolution of new technologies and the media: industry structures; media organizations; practices; representations; regulation and policy; user cultures; institutions; expertise and professions; production and consumption; leisure and work. It is important to cultivate a *historical* sense of new technologies. So I look at how both media and technology develop over time, notably: the 1980s, when digital technologies, networks and the liberalization of markets intensified alongside each other; and the 1990s, when the internet became a mass, commercial medium and broadcasting reforms gathered momentum. Finally, I take a *social-shaping* approach to technology, regarding technology as open-ended and unpredictable, but shaped by a range of forces. This is important because of the recurrent tendency to see technology as determining things – such as media. Instead I argue that technology in the media – as with technology in other domains of life – is being engaged in a complex set of interactions, the result of which cannot be prejudged.

The ideas I advance in *New Technologies and the Media* are greatly influenced by a wealth of scholarship and research, but my focus is quite specific. There are now many full-length textbooks and reference books on new media, well worth consulting (Flew, 2008; Gane and Beer, 2008; Lister, Dovey, Giddings, Grant and Kelly, 2009; Livingstone and Lievrouw, 2009; Pavlik and McIntosh, 2011). There are vast research and popular literatures on aspects of new media, including burgeoning literature on press, news, journalism and new technologies, that I draw freely upon here (Dahlgren, 2009; Fenton, 2010b; Küng, Picard and Towse, 2008; Pavlik, 2008). Online journalism and news is a growth area of research and publishing (Allan, 2006; Bruns, 2005; Meikle and Redden, 2010; Paterson and Domingo, 2008; Salwen, Garrison and Driscoll, 2005). There is a vibrant literature on alternative media (Allan and Thorsen, 2009; Atton and Hamilton, 2008; Boler, 2008). Significant books on broadcasting and new media technologies (Baltruschat, 2010; Gripsrud, 2010; Moran, 2009; Ross, 2008; Seiter, 1999) are also available. Readers of *New Technologies and the Media*, as students, teachers and researchers of the media, are warmly encouraged to familiarize themselves with these works – which offer a wealth of concepts, tools, methods and resources for critically engaging with and intervening in new technologies.

In this book, then, I aim to do two main things. First, *New Technologies and the Media* is a very short, sharp and accessible introduction to new technologies and media. Second, this book focuses on new media technologies as they relate to the 'topical' media of print, radio and television. There are very important things happening to the press, news, journalism and broadcasting in which new technologies figure very prominently. Thus *New Technologies and the Media* aims to be a succinct, critical account suitable for courses, which brings together, analyses and introduces the key concerns for media.

To provide such an introduction, the book is structured as follows, Chapter 2, 'Technology Criticism', explains the importance of taking a critical approach to technology – and how we can do this. I briefly discuss various theories of technology germane to the media, and provide an example of how to critically assess technology, using the case of the Apple iPad. I discuss the influential idea of convergence in digital technology, and show the difficulties this presents – illustrating this through the notion of formats. The remainder of the chapter concentrates on the single most important and comprehensive phenomenon in new technologies and the media at present: digital networks. I give an overview of the internet and the media cultures that have developed along with it, then briefly discuss other important networks – such as broadcasting networks, now also undergoing digital conversion and transitions. Finally, I turn to an examination of key ideas associated with digital networks – the fascination with the user, participation and the turn to personal media – before concluding with a brief discussion of mobility and mobile media.

In Chapter 3, 'What's News: The Press and New Technologies', I look at length at the internet, the technologies associated with it and their role in contemporary press transformations and challenges. I open by tracing the development of online news, with its antecedents in forms such as videotexts and early internet news. Then I discuss the broadening of news into online media from the mid-1990s to early 2000s, when newspapers were challenged, and fundamentally reshaped by developments centring on users, open systems and new media cultures. Third, I look at how the nature of news gathering, journalism and media work has changed with new technologies, discussing new kinds of new agencies, as well as the controversial WikiLeaks project. Finally, I explore the topic of mobile news, especially centring on the strategies of Rupert Murdoch's News Corporation in relation to hand-held devices such as e-readers, smartphones, tablets and iPads.

Broadcasting and new technologies form the focus of Chapter 4, 'Broadcasting Media and the Social Turn'. The chapter opens with a consideration of how new technologies played an intricate part in the development of television in the media ecologies of the household in the second half of the twentieth century. The video recorder introduced viewers to the idea of recording and playing back television, and since then we have enjoyed the technologies of the DVD, digital video recorder, media centre or server – not to mention various listening technologies. The second part of the chapter considers digital television, and how struggles were fought among contending sections of industry, government, regulators, equipment manufacturers and – to a lesser extent – communities and viewers, to gain the upper hand in influencing the future shape and social relations of television. Users have had their revenge, however, for being overlooked in digital-television developments, and, thus I conclude, with a discussion of the unpredictable ways in which users have availed themselves of internet-based technologies to reconfigure television. Here there are subtle and perhaps far-reaching logics unfolding, where the traditional idea of the broadcast relationship – from broadcaster to viewer – is being displaced by 'post-broadcast-television' ideas such as 'social television' and 'connected TV'.

In Chapter 5, 'New Associations: Technology in Media Professions and Institutions', I consider the implications that changes in media forms, practices, industries and audiences hold for the twin domains of professions and institutions. Journalism is probably the media profession most avidly discussed in recent times. I look at the populist turn (Turner, 2010) that seeks to broaden out and open up the profession of journalism. I discuss the ideas of key proponents who have been emboldened to grasp the nettle of technology's role (notably US journalism educators and scholars, Dan Gillmor and Jay Rosen) and contrast these with the range of alternative views on the state and future of journalism (such as Mark Deuze, Leopoldina Fortunati and Michael Schudson). From the profession of journalism, I move to the institution of public-sector or public-service broadcasting, which has been an important pillar of the media, and served as a foil to commercial media. Here the present wave of digital technologies has been cast – over the course of some years – as a boon to the faltering rationales of public-service media. Indeed the importance of public institutions – rather than privately owned, for-profit institutions – has emerged as a key idea in the area of the press. Thus I discuss the turn to public institutions in the area of newspapers, exploring proposals for trusts and other kinds of independent, non-profit arrangements advanced by a range of commentators as a way to underwrite the future of quality journalism in the face of the uncertain futures of commercial news outlets.

The conclusion to the book, Chapter 6, 'New Media Concerns', argues that new technologies have seen the reinvigoration of long-standing concerns in media. In addition, with new technologies we have in process the creation of an extensive set of novel concerns: from intellectual property, new dimensions of access and equity, through to the enlargement of media to encompass previously unmediated domains of everyday life. Such concerns, old and new, all underscore the need to take a critical stance on new technologies, the underlying theme of the book with which I will begin.

2 Technology Criticism

Governments of the Industrial World, you weary giants of flesh and steel, I come from Cyberspace, the new home of Mind. On behalf of the future, I ask you of the past to leave us alone … . Cyberspace does not lie within your borders … . We are forming our own Social Contract … . We are creating a world where anyone, anywhere may express his or her beliefs, no matter how singular, without fear of being coerced into silence or conformity.

John Perry Barlow, 'A Declaration of the Independence of Cyberspace' (Barlow, 1996)

'New' media technologies as we know them, and all of their components, are defined by their own decomposition … . Billions of pieces of computers, Internet hardware, cell phones, portable music devices, and countless other consumer electronics have already been trashed or await their turn. The entire edifice of new communications technology is a giant heap waiting to happen, a monument to the hubris of computing and the peculiar shape of digital capitalism.

(Sterne, 2007, p. 17)

In less than seven years, [Mark] Zuckerberg wired together a twelfth of humanity into a single network, thereby creating a social entity almost twice as large as the US. If Facebook were a country it would be the third largest, behind only China and India … . We are now running our social lives through a for-profit network that, on paper at least, has made Zuckerberg a billionaire six times over.

(Grossman, 2010)

Technology has long underpinned media. There are technologies used by journalists for capturing and representing news: the pen and reporter's notepad; the system of shorthand; the newspaper and the printing press; the camera. Technologies for filing stories or copy, or conveying images: the telegraph; telephone; satellite systems.

Technologies for distributing media: the transport and distribution systems that deliver newspapers, magazines, books and printed materials directly to newsagents and news stands, book stores or readers themselves; the transmission systems and receivers that allow broadcasting to occur, with television being beamed from towers or satellites – and through cable-subscription systems – to TV sets and viewers.

From time to time, technology change has caused disruption, upset, excitement, even revolution in media. The telegraph allowed the dissemination of news across vast distances very quickly. The invention of photography saw the visual image develop a critical role in the illustration of newspaper and magazine stories, and then genres, practices and an identity of its own – photojournalism. With the invention of the moving image came cinema as an important form of media, including 'newsreel' stories for cinemagoing audiences, and television as a medium that revolves around the visual, and its interplay with words, sounds and other images. Orbiting satellites allowed television to be watched by millions of viewers, with new dimensions of 'liveness' being created.

What is significant about the present moment – indeed the rationale for this book – is that the question of technology has assumed a cardinal importance for the very definition of media. Many of the current debates about media – its characteristics, social functions, cultural meanings and futures – pivot on technology. Technology is vitally involved in the transformation of media and communications. It is not simply restricted to one particular standalone machine, or application, or media gadget or device. There is a very intensive, widespread and far-reaching set of technological systems undergoing profound change, with media experiencing some of the most direct effects of any area of society. Two words can suffice to indicate the magnitude of this shift: the internet. Later, I will explain the internet as a technological system, and why it carries so many consequences for the nature of the media. (Interestingly the seventh edition of a standard media work on the media is now entitled *Power without Responsibility: Press, Broadcasting and the Internet in Britain*; see Curran and Seaton, 2010). At this stage, it is simply worth noting that the internet affects virtually every area of contemporary media. And while it is the most salient and decisive technology for media currently, it is certainly not the only such disruptive, consolidating or controlling technology at present.

Despite the centrality of technology in media now, what technology is, and the role it plays in media concerns, remains obscure. For many people, technology is difficult to understand, because of its specialized, technical and scientific aura. It is hard to follow, because the pace of technological change is so fast. Worse still, technology is regarded as a given. We are often told that things happen because of technology. The implication of this being that we cannot alter the direction of technology, so instead we need to modify our own lives to accommodate or work around it.

Thus technology rouses many emotions and affects. Some people profess to love technology. They adore new gadgets and are happy to stand in line to be the first to buy the new device from a funky technology company. By the same token, quite a sizeable portion of the population is fearful of, resistant to or nonplussed, concerning technology and the change it represents. Instead, many people are more comfortable continuing to use technologies no longer seen as 'modern', fashionable or efficient. Quite some go further and believe that many new technologies have detrimental effects, bringing undesirable changes to a wide range of phenomena affecting the nature of personal interaction and communication, friendships and family relationships, the quality of public conversations, workplaces, intimacy and sexuality, or cross the boundaries between public and private lives in distinctively unwelcome ways.

Because of the very visible, contradictory and even controversial place of technology in our everyday lives with media, I would like to start in this chapter to establish a basic understanding of technology, how we can approach it and what kinds of things we can expect of it (as well as what we cannot). First, I present the idea that to understand media we really need to adopt a critical stance towards technology. Second, I give a brief overview of key technologies affecting the press and broadcasting, revolving around the salience of networks in the dynamics around new technology and media.

Takes on Technology

If we stop to define technology, we discover it to be a much wider and richer topic than often thought. The word has a complicated history, but it comes from the combination of the ancient Greek τέχνο (techno-) plus –λογία (-logy). As its entry in the *Oxford English Dictionary* outlines, the word τεχνολογία is used in Hellenistic Greek, to mean systematic treatment (particularly applied to grammar); after that it appears in the early seventh century in a treatise of the liberal arts as the Latin word *technologia* (*Oxford English Dictionary*, 2010). One thousand years on, it can be traced in French in the mid-seventeenth century (*technologie*) and German (*Technologie*) one hundred years or so after that, when it gains its sense of meaning 'the branch of knowledge dealing with the mechanical arts and applied sciences'. In the early nineteenth century, 'technology' gains an additional meaning of 'the application of such knowledge for practical purposes'. Finally at the dawn of the twenty-first century, it gains the sense by which most of us best know it: 'The product of such application [of knowledge]; technological knowledge or know-how; a technological process, method, or technique. Also: machinery, equipment, etc., developed from the practical application of scientific and technical knowledge ...' (*Oxford English Dictionary*, 2010).

As Andrew Ross notes, '[m]odern shifts in the meaning of technology ... clearly reflect the rise of industrialization and the onset of economic development tied to science-based innovations' (Ross, 2005, p. 342). Ross argues that by the nineteenth century:

> science-based invention had become the driving force behind capitalist growth, and technology was increasingly used to refer to the machinery itself ... . [By the 1970s and 1980s] developments in the fields of micro-electronics and biotechnology generated mass production of high technology ... and vernacular [that is, use of the term 'technology' is increasingly identified with these material artifacts.
>
> (Ross, 2005, p. 343)

So we can see that 'technology' has a wide range of meanings and can be applied to many things. Yet the word also conveys very strong, narrow associations about things that are practically and symbolically important to our societies (Winner, 1986).

An awareness of the linguistic and historical evolution of the term 'technology' is helpful as we begin to develop a critical framework. The approach to technology I favour draws upon social, cultural and political understandings from a number of overlapping schools or tendencies. These different approaches to studying technology each have their own histories, methods and biases, and include science and technology studies, social construction of technology (Bijker, Hughes and Pinch, 1987), social shaping of technology (MacKenzie and Wajcman, 1985; Williams and Edge, 1996), domestication theory (discussed below), accounts of sociotechnical systems, actor-network-theory (Latour, 2005; Law and Hassard, 1999) and others. What is common to these ways of thinking about technology from the 1970s onwards is the idea of redressing the balance between science and technology, and society. For at least three decades, scholars have sought to understand the social dimension of technology, with many believing that it needs to be restored to its rightful place – and others (notably influential French theorist of technology Bruno Latour) arguing that a proper appreciation of technology means we have to entirely rethink – indeed reassemble – our idea of what society, and the social, is. The upshot of this intense research and debate upon technology across the humanities and social sciences, as well as sciences, in recent years is that we have tremendous conceptual resources for better understanding how technology and media come together – the theme to which I'll now return.

We still tend to credit developers, scientists, engineers and entrepreneurs with the achievement of the invention of a new technology. Invention actually involves a set of entangled processes of discovery, forgetting and rediscovery, imagination and implementation. The intended recipients (often seen as beneficiaries) also play an important role in the definition of technology. We have a well-known example synonymous with the wholesale rejection of technology: the Luddites (Jones, 2006). These were a group of workers several decades into the 'Industrial Revolution' in England, led by Ned Ludd, who destroyed the frames (or new machine for weaving) being introduced into their traditional work. Such machines were harbingers of novel modes of work and social organization, in the form of factories. The fight of the Luddites – misunderstood as a group of people standing against technology (believed to be synonymous with progress) – can make us sensitive to paying attention to how people react to, receive, incorporate, celebrate and tame technology (Grint and Woolgar, 1997; Slack and Wise, 2005; Thompson, 1963). As historian E. P. Thompson observed of the Luddite movement: 'We must see through the machine-breaking to the motives of the men wielding the hammers ... one is struck not so much by its backwardness as by its growing maturity' (Thompson, 1963, p. 601).

If nothing else, the recent work of scholars in the fields of social studies of science establishes the existence of strong forces that shape technology, but also its constitutive and surprising unpredictability. A particular technology can have a very peculiar and unpredictable career. This can be glimpsed in the variegated fortunes of technical standards. The width of train lines, called the 'gauge', varies not only between countries, but among the provinces or states of the countries themselves. In Australia, the adjoining states of New South Wales and Queensland still operate on train lines with different gauges, so engines have to be halted, and adjustments made after a border crossing. When it came to early videotapes, for instance, the VHS format enjoyed vastly greater success worldwide than did the Sony Betamax format. Different countries often choose different standards – Europe chose PAL for television transmission, the US chose NTSC. The uncertain trajectories – or 'biographies' – of particular technologies are worth bearing in mind, as too is the idea that a range of factors shape technologies and technological systems.

This is revealed by another useful approach to understanding technology, namely the 'domestication' approach, associated with Roger Silverstone and Leslie Haddon (Berker, 2006; Haddon, 2006; Silverstone and Haddon, 1996; Silverstone, Hirsch and Morley, 1992), which studies how users 'tame' technology, making it part of their lives and finding new uses for it. There are many such examples we can call to mind, such as the mobile phone – which is literally taken apart, put back together, thrown around, dropped, adorned and decorated, upgraded, customized and recycled, by its users (Hjorth, 2009). Larissa Hjorth has shown the ways in which such customization of mobile phones, and indeed technology generally, is deeply gendered as revealed in cases in Hong Kong and Japan where young women, for instance, often instruct their boyfriends on the art of adorning one's phone (Hjorth, 2009).

Such critical frameworks help us regard technology as an open set of questions – as a problematic – not as a given. This is helpful when we confront the other important way that technology is typically presented now (as in the title of this book). When it comes to media, and much else besides, there is an emphasis on technology being *new*. An excellent first step in analysis is to question what exactly is 'new' about a technology that is breathlessly, and even in a considered manner, being presented as novel.

To give a concrete example of the politics and perils of the 'new', let us take a case that we will encounter later in the book: the Apple iPad. In mid-2010, Apple Corporation launched its much anticipated device to great fanfare. What was new about this technology? At first blush, the novelty lies in Apple iPad's differentiating itself from other kinds of devices and media technologies, signifying something different. Reminiscent of the Apple iPhone, the iPad refreshes the company reputation for sleek design with the notion that this device is not a laptop computer exactly, nor a mobile phone. The iPad conceivably allows this, as we saw from the case of the Norwegian Prime Minister, Jens Stoltenberg, stuck in New York owing to the volcanic ash cloud causing the cancellation of air travel, running his country from his brand-new

iPad – an image of which was proudly posted on the gov
cial Flickr account (*Huffington Post*, 2010). Yet the iPad is fir
most calibrated with the habits of the media *consumer*, rath
producer (or at least office business market type), in mind. The iPa
can read her newspaper, view photos in glorious resolution and colou
watch movies and play games, with a thing that can be comfortably
used in the bedroom, plane, train or bus, or in domestic or work
settings. At least this is the way that the iPad has been mostly represented in Apple's advertising and promotional material, in media coverage, in specialized technology circles, blogs and journals, and in the
digital culture and lifestyle coverage that now appears in mainstream
media. Yet what is really 'new' about the iPad is still quite unclear.

After all, the idea of reading has been with us for many centuries, and
the book, magazine, newspaper and pamphlet have their own histories.
Computers have at least a seventy-year history, and have been in
portable devices like mobile phones or portable gameplayers since the
early 1990s. Portable digital assistants, laptop computers, notebook
computers and 'tablet' computers have all proliferated. Electronic book
readers themselves have been available since at least the turn of the
twenty-first century, but increasingly since 2006 with the Sony E-reader
(with e-ink), and then since Amazon launched its Kindle in 2008. In
2011, there exists an array of e-reader devices, functioning across hardware, software and different networks.

So the iPad combines and reanimates a throng of existing meanings
about media, well-established (even antique), as well as much newer
practices of use and consumption, not to mention predecessor technologies as much as those of the present day. What the iPad signifies is
produced from all these things. It is partly a function of where it sits in
this shifting strata of media histories, and partly an outcome of its
differences from other media technologies in the present – rather like
trying to ascertain what is new about a word in the face of the dynamic
nature of language. Further still, the meanings – and fates – of the iPad
are still not ultimately known. Is it a 'success'? For whom, where, for
what purposes and in what contexts? Is it simply yet another 'new'
technology that viewed one year, ten years, 100 years, 1,000 years on,
was not as important as thought? Or, rather, was its eventually unre-
markable character actually exemplary in a different way?

This brief study of the iPad reminds us to beware of the prophets
proclaiming false gods, especially when it comes to technology, when
all is definitively and magically new. As a counter to this permanent
novelty, we need to study each technology carefully to ascertain what is

what it carries over or borrows from
ects that precede it, and to determine
recasts, what we understand as media. It
:he new if we are alive to various accounts
nat imagine different ways of conceiving
of media and technology are an excellent
)n theories that wish to overturn discussion
old and new media, dead media, renewing
Last but certainly not least, there is research
that urges ..   :h broader and deeper perspectives on what
technologies of media ..ctually are, so expanding our horizons of
thought.

With these framing remarks concerning new technology (hopefully
allaying the concerns of readers not usually enamoured with it), I will
turn to a brief guided tour of the main technologies involved in print
and broadcasting media. The most central and avidly discussed technology it is still useful – for a little while longer at least – to call digital technology. Much media change and accompanying concerns still relate to
the complicated processes surrounding digitalization, and the
protracted, messy shift from 'analogue' technologies to 'digital' ones,
and the interplay of convergence and divergence. Many of the technologies involved in media are already digital in nature, and are now
being replaced, re-engineered, or combining with new technologies.
The digital nature of technologies is still important to understanding
the fundamental nature of what is perceived as 'new' in technologies
affecting media today, so I will stick with this rubric.

Digital Forms and Formats

The phenomenon of digitalization has been with us for the past two
decades, and well underway for much longer than this. Simply put, the
stuff of media – words, texts, images, sounds, sensations and design –
can be converted to a stream of ones and zeros (binary code). This
fundamental encoding of what otherwise is non-digital (often referred
to as 'analogue') into digital form has profound implications. It allows
media to be stored, transmitted, communicated, retrieved, inspected
and enjoyed across what were thought to be previously distinct areas of
the media. This is especially the case when we consider the domain of
production, long considered to be distinct from the distribution and
consumption of media.

Take, for instance, the equipment used by media professionals, producers and workers. Newspaper journalists traditionally sought information, researched stories, conducted interviews and sought to witness and report events first-hand. They wrote up, compiled or constructed their stories, and filed them. Copy was sub-edited, laid out in newspapers and printed. Now the locales and cultures of newspaper production have radically changed, and digital technology is involved in many parts of this. Journalists use computers, rather than typewriters, to write their stories. Newsrooms themselves have been reconfigured, under rubrics of 'digital', 'online', or 'convergent' newsrooms. While the topic of new technology as it relates to changes in production of media and production cultures is a highly significant discussion in its own right, what is notable now is how this is bound up with debates about the distribution and consumption of media. I will return to this topic shortly – in order to appreciate the saturation of the nature, contexts and places of media production by digital technologies – for the present we need to understand a little about the important part that formats play in creating the categories, organization and pathways for digital forms.

A myth associated with digital technologies is that once something analogue is encoded in digital form, or, better still according to proponents of this form, 'born digital' (that is, created from the beginning as digital data), then it is possible for it to be stored, manipulated, remixed, mashed-up and transported across quite different kinds of equipment, devices, screens and output medium. The myth of seamless digital interchangeability is at the heart of the untroubled notion of convergence. This myth suggests that, with these new digital technologies, hitherto distinct media, their styles of production and consumption, their long-developed cultures and industries, can be quickly fused together. If thoroughly discredited in reality, convergence remains a potent myth governing understanding of new technologies and the media, so it is important we pause to interrogate it. In order to assist us, it is useful to consider the concept of formats.

It is certainly the case that with the right software and equipment, a media form can be transferred across formats: music can be recorded, edited, remixed and listened to across vinyl records, compact discs (CDs), MP3s, iTunes and other media. Photos can be transferred from a print created from chemical and paper-based development to digital formats. Or images can originate from different cameras – still or movie cameras, mobile phones or cameras installed in computers – and be saved or transferred in different photographic or moving-picture formats, destined to be displayed, transmitted or recombined in quite different contexts: albums, Facebook pages, websites, photo-sharing websites, digital frames in households, mobile phones, multiple screens and editing software and various portable digital devices. Television offers an excellent example of the impact of the advent of digitalization, with digital video displacing videocam recorders, which in turn modified and change professional-level television camerawork. The fact that the very identity of television is now in question – spanning broadcast and cable television through new forms of digital television to internet downloading of television programmes and YouTube – points to the malleability of digital images.

Yet as we realize by analogy with the case of languages and the possibility both of translation and its incommensurability, formats are hard-fought, highly constructed artefacts in their own right. Formats function as ways to frame media material and content, and appropriations of information. It is important to recognize how particular digital formats work, and what kinds of choice of materials they make – including some kinds of information, and excluding other types. Formats share many things with technical standards: they are the results of negotiation, battles of actors and industries, and accidents of time and place. Once settled, formats then suggest and become aligned with particular kinds of media uses, preferences and meanings – thus are often integrally involved in new media cultures. Thus formats are cultural achievements in their own right.

A well-known example is the MP3 format, the signature format of digital music (displaced a little perhaps by Apple's iTunes Plus format). Jonathan Sterne has provided a persuasive account of how the format itself is conjoined with leading features of portable music, its consumption and listening (Sterne, 2012). Of the MP3, Sterne writes:

> The mp3 is a crystallized set of social and material relations. It is an item that 'works for' and is 'worked on' by a host of people, ideologies, technologies and other social and material elements ... the mp3 [is] an artifact shaped by several electronics industries, the recoding industry and actual and idealized practices of listening.
>
> (Sterne, 2006, p. 826)

The case of the MP3 and other digital audio and music formats illustrates the point that a great deal hangs upon the actual forms that digital technologies take. These forms neither fall out of the air, so to speak, nor are they simple extensions of an abstract principle of digital ontology. They are embedded in social, political, cultural, economic, linguistic and other dynamics, through which media are produced and reproduced.

Canny Networks

Thus the novelty in technologies concerning media remains significantly bound up with digitalization and the particular affordances of digital technologies as well as the ways in which these are being hooked up, and combining into, distinctively new, if still inchoate and unstable, media ecologies. As we have seen already, these digital technologies operate very much in relation to each other – not least because the contents, applications and services that comprise contemporary media are able to – or indeed need to – work across platforms, because of the characteristics of digital transfer, files, formats, storage and retrieval. Yet the process of achieving digital technologies and their convergence is actually a messy, complicated, politically loaded and historically contingent affair. Armed with this knowledge, we can turn to consider perhaps the cardinal feature of new technologies today, and one also bound up with digitalization: networks. Digital technologies, especially in the case of media, are increasingly tied into various sorts of overlapping communication data networks.

The most pervasive and perhaps most dynamic of these networks is the internet. The most obvious reason why the internet dominates the media landscape presently is that it has the ability to span many protocols, technologies, media and networks. Developed in the 1960s, the internet commenced in 1969 connecting a number of US universities. What defines the internet in technical terms is that it is a set of protocols – specifically, the TCP/IP (transmission control protocol/internet protocol) protocols. Leaving aside a technical discussion, the internet works by allowing packets of data to be transmitted around a network. An item, such as an email, message or file, is taken apart, and put into many small packets of data. The packets are given headers (labelled with information about their contents and addresses) and each is despatched. The packets often take different routes across different networks, but they are reassembled at their destination. The beauty of the internet lies in the fact that the protocols allow it to work across different kinds of networks. Especially in the 1970s and 1980s, the internet was simply an infant among many other older, more developed computer or telecommunications data networks. Phone companies, in particular, were developing a range of standards and protocols for data networking, but eventually the internet become more and more widely used.

Through the 1990s, especially after the invention of the World Wide Web in the late 1980s, the internet popularized online communications (as data networking became known). Private networks aimed at the household or consumer markets, such as America Online (AOL), CompuServe and others, had developed their own proprietary standards, as had the various telecommunications companies that offered computer networking. In France, for instance, the state provided a pioneering online service called Minitel (Marchand, 1987; Organization for Economic Cooperation and Development, 1998), which preceded the popular diffusion of the internet by quite some years.

By the end of the 1990s (its third official decade), the internet was firmly established as the reigning network. A decade later, as champagne corks popped in honour of the internet's fourth decade, telecommunications networks around the world were well on the way to being redefined as internet protocol networks. The 'next-generation' networks in which the telecommunications companies were investing trillions of dollars were no longer based on the classic principles of telephony established over a century before (in technical terms what is called 'circuit-switched' networks). These next-generation networks were digital, internet-based networks, based on 'packet-switching'. The magnitude of the switch can be measured by the fact that 124 million subscribers in the first half of 2010 were using Skype (Skype, 2010), the so-called voice and video over internet protocol services provided by the popular company. By comparison, in the same year 1.197 billion subscribers clung onto their classic fixed-line phone services provided by the telecommunications networks (International Telecommunications Union, 2010).

As well as operating famously as a 'network of networks', the internet contains an expanding universe of many applications, programs and technologies, each having its own characteristics and user cultures. One can speak of the 'internet', and, as we have noticed, it has its technical definitions. The 'internet' also carries with it another meaning as a technology and media form. It is associated, for instance, with ideas of freedom. Often, the coupling of the internet with freedom, democracy and open markets rather resembles the structure of a myth or indeed what has long been called an 'ideology' (Sarikakis and Thussu, 2006). The internet has been associated with media freedom, and there has been much written about the contribution that the internet makes to democracy (Chadwick and Howard, 2008; Coleman, 2009; Hindman,

2009; Shiller, 2005). Further, and perhaps more clearly as an ideology, the internet is seen as synonymous with free markets themselves (Shiller, 2005). We can find a nice example of this in the former British Prime Minister Tony Blair's memoir. In order to clinch a point about the backwardness of his antagonists on the conservative Tory side of politics, as well as in his own Labour Party, Blair evokes the transformations that new technology have wrought: 'All around the globe, the new technology – the internet, computers, mobile phones, mass travel and communication – was opening the world up, casting people together, mixing cultures, races, faiths in a vast melting pot of human interaction' (Blair, 2010).

The origins of such ideologies lie in the myths that were associated with the rise of the internet in the 1990s in the US (Friedman, 2005; Turner, 2006). Here the internet was imagined as a zone for a narrow yet powerfully influential set of North American myths – the digital equivalent of *pax americana*. We can see this myth of the internet, as promoted by enthusiasts such as John Perry Barlow, Mitch Kapor, the Electronic Frontiers Foundation and the groovy cyberculture magazine that defined this period of the internet's rising stakes in fashionable culture – *Wired* magazine (Flichy, 2007). Or with the limitless possibilities of technology and their capacity to achieve a metamorphosis of life as we know it, the subject of much work around design and technology famously captured in MIT Lab's Nicholas Negroponte's classic mid-1990s book *Being Digital* (Negroponte, 1995). The internet had to do with cyberspace, a term lifted from the fictions of William Gibson (Gibson, 1984, 1986), and, like the Wild West in the nineteenth century, it was imagined as an ungovernable frontier place with its own sovereignty where laws did not apply (Barlow, 1996; Paasonen, 2009). These myths about freedom and an arena which escaped the reach of government was coloured by the role that counterculture played in the early notions of virtual online communities, exemplified by Howard Rheingold's avidly read *Virtual Communities* (Rheingold, 1993; Turner, 2006). The idea that the internet was another world – a virtual world – still weighs heavily on how technology is popularly viewed (Malaby, 2009; Turkle, 1995). In three-dimensional, online, 'immersive', worlds, where users can obviously play with identities such as *Second Life*, there is an explicit construction of other worlds – or at least, a doubling of this one in which we live (Boellstorff, 2008; Hillis, 2009; Hillis and Petit, 2006; Malaby, 2009).

Allied to myths of the internet role's in media, political and social freedom are other potent ideas about the technology's role in creating new forms of value and indeed economic system. Towards the end of the 1990s, there was a widespread belief that companies operating on the internet defied the rules of traditional economic gravity. We were living in a 'new economy', in which companies such as Amazon.com, or many other companies which rose briefly to prominence by virtue of using the internet in innovative ways, did not need to make a profit (Kelly, 1998; Löfgren and Willim, 2005). The fact that such start-ups achieved stratospheric demand for their stock with their initial public offerings (IPOs) conferred a warrant for the fate of a company's costs and revenues thereafter. Of course, I overstate the case for purposes of emphasis, these were heady times indeed. The high-water mark of this 'dot.com' fever was marked by the take-over of the mammoth media entertainment company Time Warner by computer networking-cum-internet company AOL in 2000. Since the dot.com bust – what Geert Lovink ironically referred to as the internet darlings' 'first recession' (Lovink, 2003) – the relationship between the internet and economics has been recognized as far more complex than that assumed by the initial flush of entrepreneurial enthusiasm and speculation. However, there is no doubt that the internet has brought significant changes to business and economics (Aspray and Ceruzzi, 2008), especially enlarging the area of economics when it comes to media. We will discuss this later on in relation to Web 2.0; for the present I note that media is no longer confined to its traditional areas. It has expanded to cover the areas of mediatization of interpersonal and group communications via the internet. Media has also expanded to take a claim in the booming area of trade in services. For example, eBay is a widely used trading site for buying and selling all sorts of goods and services. It is a consumer and cultural phenomenon in its own right (Hillis and Petit, 2006). As well as being embedded in everyday or popular culture, commercial transactional sites such as eBay are deeply entwined in the operations of global media companies. Another instance of development in the internet with implications for how we approach media and economics lies in the fact that online worlds, from *Second Life* to online gaming, have their own forms of labour as well as leisure – what Julian Kücklich dubs 'playbour' (Kücklich, 2005). These new forms of work are embedded in online economies that have material links to offline economies (Castranova, 2005; Malaby, 2009) – not least through the obvious mechanism of an exchange rate.

So far I have talked about what characterizes the internet in technical terms, and also some of the *ideés fortes* (powerful ideas) that have shaped dominant understandings of the technology. What is evident as we delve into 'the internet' – like inspecting a fractal or organism under a microscope – is that it actually comprises many component parts, each with its own cultures, effects and meanings. Add to this that the singular internet has developed very differently across the world, so that what we often refer to as 'the internet' is actually a collection of quite different and peculiar 'internets' (Goggin, 2011a).

First let us consider the internet as a bewildering array of specific technologies. The internet refers to communications, information and media technologies delivered by networks using the suite of protocols termed internet protocol for ease of reference. Like other networks, from a technical perspective the internet is comprised of different 'layers': applications, transport, networks and links (Clarke, Dempsey, Nee and O'Connor, 1998). Important for our purposes of understanding the internet as global media is the applications layer. The applications layer includes long-standing protocols, such as those used: to provide web services (Hypertext Transfer Protocol, or HTTP), email (Simple Mail Transfer Protocol, or SMTP), and file transfer (File Transfer Protocol, or FTP). One of the early applications developed for the internet – and still the most enduring (if often vexing) – is electronic mail.

Email allowed users of the computer terminals connected together through the internet to communicate with each other. Eventually email developed into a massive communications technology in its own right. Email also allowed many-to-many communication, through things such as email lists and listservers (unknown to many denizens for whom Facebook is, temporarily at least, the alpha and omega, but beloved of the author who proudly admits to being an internet dinosaur). Applications emerged to allow internet users to share files among themselves, but also to upload these to central nodes in the network, where they could be searched for and downloaded by others (using programs such as ftp, Veronica and others). Users devised early online networked games, and also multi-user spaces, such as MUDs (Multi User Dungeon) and MOOs (MUD, object-oriented), all predecessors to the online chat rooms as well as immersive virtual worlds that we now take for granted. Finally, but certainly not exhaustively in the text-based world of internet, were newsgroups, which allowed people to share information, news and files (see Chapter 3).

Two developments in the early 1990s were key to the internet's transformation from a medium difficult to use for many beyond small groups of adherents to the global media system it is today. The World Wide Web was invented, and by 1992–3 a 'browser' was developed to make it easy to put up, find and retrieve information on the internet

(Berners-Lee and Fischetti, 1999; Cailliau, 2000). The impact of this was magnified by the release of Microsoft's Windows operating system, and software that thereafter relied heavily on graphical-user interfaces to represent and navigate information and applications. In the two decades since the early 1990s, the number of significant internet applications has expanded ceaselessly (Brugger, 2010). The World Wide Web has remained foundational as something that has dramatically changed the way media works, because, like the internet, the Web bridges and combines various underlying programs, technologies and network architectures. Especially with 'plug-ins', new programs can simply be added to the user's browser that relatively seamlessly incorporate new functionality in one's desktop. There are whole new realms of technology that are proving decisive for the kind of media discussed in this book. As this is a vast area, I will briefly discuss but three here: blogs; peer-to-peer filesharing; and social media.

Blogs are relatively straightforward as a technical development in the internet. Emerging as 'web logs' (thus the contraction 'blogs'), or thought of first as web diaries, blogs rely on features of the World Wide Web to offer an architecture for regular comment, that can be easily updated, widely distributed and commented upon via others. Blogs can be easily linked with other blogs (through blogrolls) and also with other applications (websites, social media). The significance of the blog for media lies in its galvanizing a new genre for offering commentary, opinion and debate. Aggregated together in a parallel world called the 'blogosphere', blogs have become an integral part of the public spheres in many countries, and indeed mainstream media (Bruns and Jacobs, 2006). Blogs are easy to establish and maintain, and so are a low-cost, flexible, simple form of independent media – and offer a platform for distribution that has relatively very low barriers to entry. Especially in countries with limited media freedom, blogs have often played an enormously important role in publishing and circulating news, opinion and commentary. Hence blogs have been celebrated in countries such as Iran (Srebeny and Khiabany, 2010) or China (Russell and Echchaibi, 2009), and from the right-wing as well as the left-wing, have been influential across many countries not least the US and Europe (Tremayne, 2007).

Peer-to-peer (p2p) filesharing applications have been around for quite some time, beginning with early applications for filesharing in the text-based internet. Peer-based networks assumed a much, much greater cultural importance with the advent of Napster, Kazaa, Grokster, BitTorrent and other widely used applications. While music was the media form most initially affected (David, 2010), television quickly became affected – because users would bypass traditional modes of media distribution and consumption (Noam and Pupillo, 2008). Instead of relying on a television broadcaster to schedule or replay a programme, or a video recorder to create a tape for subsequent viewing, viewers recorded programmes, converted these into suitable digital form (a process made very easy with digital television), and via p2p applications made them available for sharing by millions of users around the world.

Blogs and p2p are forerunners of a much more pervasive phenomenon on the internet often called social media. All media has a *social* function, however what is accented in the term 'social media' is a new group of internet technologies, which rely upon – indeed are constituted by – the productive interactions of media consumers and users. In the case of p2p technologies, there is no point in launching a program such as BitTorrent or Kazaa unless someone has already uploaded content to the network of nodes that comprise it. As users download a video, music clip, book or image from such a network, and, as long as they consent to it, they are simultaneously making it available for downloading from their computer by another user. In a different fashion with a blog, there is a clear authorial or producer function, even if collective or multi-authored, yet the role of the audience as listeners and interlocutors is heightened.

The term social media began to be used to describe not only collaborative projects, or peer-to-peer sharing or content, or the conversational, accretive form of blogs, but new phenomena. Social bookmarking, for instance, is a practice where people browsing the web bookmark and tag a website not simply for their own purposes, or browser, but using an application such as Delicious or digg that allows them to share their bookmarks with small or large groups of other users. The extraordinary rise of social-networking systems, such as Facebook, is also seen by many as a form of social media. It is a way to keep in touch with family, friends, colleagues and indeed anyone else who might share one's interests. However, it relies upon the Facebook user sharing information, photos or other content about themselves, then engaging in social practices of interaction with their network of Facebook users. The video-sharing site YouTube is another example of social media, ostensibly born from users' desires to watch or upload video, but now from this sharing of content, and interactions around that (such as the creation of fan communities), creating a distinctive new media form, which has shifted the boundaries of television, video and film.

An obvious attribute of social media is its hybridity. The short-messaging broadcast application Twitter – loved and loathed by turns –

allows sharing of content and weblinks, especially through a program that abbreviates the web address (such as Tiny URL). Social-media applications and types have proliferated to the extent that applications exist to bring many of them together into the same program (Friendfeed, Plaxo) or device (plug-ins for browsers or operating systems on phones such as the iPhone). It is difficult to claim any precision for the term 'social media', but for the present it does at least indicate the most discussed, dynamic area of internet culture. Like the internet generally, social media is increasingly embedded within, displacing, overrunning, pre-empting or bypassing, established media – especially, as we shall discuss later, when it comes to news.

Many Other Networks Besides

The internet is a veritable network of networks. It also interacts with many other non-internet-based networks. For our purposes, various sorts of analogue and digital-transmission networks hold the utmost importance for the future of broadcasting in television and radio.

From approximately the middle of the twentieth century, television has assumed a relatively settled form of distribution and consumption. Television programmes are compiled, then 'broadcast' via transmitter over radio waves, to be received and displayed on receivers, or television sets. There have been three main forms of television broadcast: terrestrial (broadcast across the surface of the earth by transmitters); satellite (television beamed from broadcast studios to satellites, and then broadcast by satellites across a territory where households equipped with satellite dishes can receive the signal); and cable (television transmitted via cables in conduits underground, or on electricity poles, to subscribers). For much of its existence television broadcasting involved analogue transmission. Since at least the 1970s, it has been possible to encode programme material in digital form (Abramson, 2003). Once these technologies became widely used, they allowed the digital transmission of this digital content. Thus broadcasting networks themselves have become increasingly digitalized. Existing cable networks can be used to transmit signal in digital forms. So too can spectrum. With new broadcasting equipment, and facilities, channels can be bundled together, and broadcast to viewers. For their part, viewers require new digital television receivers capable of receiving and decoding these new transmissions, and displaying them on screens.

Digital television has been in planning for many years. Its promoters have claimed several virtues for it, such as higher resolution, more efficient use of scarce spectrum (Stafford, 1980), as well as increased ability for viewers to interact with content, combine channels on the one screen or retrieve more information on television programmes. In most countries, digital television has been slow to start, causing governments and regulators to set dates for the switch-off of analogue television and the switch-over to digital television (2012 in the UK or, in many other territories, 2020). Because of the cost of buying new television receivers, dealing with incompatibility and coverage issues, as well as learning how to use the new sets and services, it has been necessary for governments to create substantial digital switch-over programs. In addition, the introduction of digital broadcasting has been accompanied by major policy debates about the so-called 'digital dividend'. With the advent of digital television comes the freeing up of spectrum, previously needed for analogue television's greater bandwidth needs.

As it turns out, spectrum holds the keys to the kingdom of future media. Many new technologies from broadcasting through wireless internet and mobiles to new sensing, car-navigation and radio-frequency identification (RFID) technologies require spectrum in order to operate. Consequently there is much pressure upon spectrum allocation, but only so many radio waves in a given location and atmosphere that can be used. The realization that digital television carries with it a chance for governments and their publics to think about who should have access to vacated spectrum, for what valued future services, for whom, at what price, with what economic, social and cultural implications, is precisely what triggered intense debate about this historical opportunity.

In the realm of broadcasting, the trajectory of digital radio (or digital audio broadcasting) has been obscured and relatively neglected – at least in comparison with its televisual cousin. While digital television has come from a slow start, and involved a fierce battle over standards and the general worth of a new, expensive technology and household equipment makeover, it has at least been roundly endorsed by governments, industry and, dragged along for the ride, viewers. In contrast, digital radio has not received such backing from government. Digital radio has been something of a success in the United Kingdom, which has had the world's biggest network. Digital audio broadcasting has flourished in Britain, with listeners appreciating the quality of signal and the new range of stations, programmes and material on offer – and AM and FM radio are set to migrate to digital by 2015. Elsewhere, however, regulators have been reluctant to mandate either the introduction of digital radio, or weight the terms of this transition towards those of the new interests promoting the technology (by dint of closing down the analogue network). So digital radio has been slowly developed and eventually launched, and has attracted a band of appreciative adherents (O'Neill, 2010). Yet to the untrained ear of many a listener, digital radio does not yet offer a great advance over its analogue counterpart. (Just before Christmas in 2009, the author went to a local audio and hi-fi specialist to purchase a digital radio, and, despite sets being offered in the store, was so dispirited by the proprietor's inveighing against the inferior listening experience of the new technology that he eventually gave up and slouched out empty-handed). In addition, digital radio broadcasting in its official radio-industry sanctioned and developed forms has lumbered along in the wake of the explosion of informal and formal digital radio varieties (Eble and Gunnel, 2006) – part of a broader phenomenon in how broadcasting really has been reshaped to which I will now turn.

Until quite recently, it was assumed that the future trajectory of television and radio respectively would be bound up with the digital broadcasting standards, equipment and spectrum battles that we have just considered. Now, however, it is painfully obvious that digital broadcasting does not stand on its own feet. In the richer countries, media industries are investing in next-generation, ultra-high bandwidth broadband networks. These are networks that will be based on internet protocol, but also on very high data capacity and transfer rates – especially to support the steadily increasing use of video communications. While there is a range of networks and technologies that already provides quite high data rates, and might do in the future, the already available technology that is regarded as 'future proof' (or at least having a relatively distant horizon as far as can be conceived at this stage) is optical fibre.

A slender cable made of glass, fibre optic allows transmission at nearly the speed of light, and can carry what are regarded now as amazing amounts of data. The rub is that fibre optic, being a cable-based technology, needs ideally to be buried underground in conduits. This requires relatively expensive excavation and installation, and the accompanying node and network equipment. Nonetheless many countries believe fibre optic to the home, or very nearby, is the best way to invest in communications infrastructure. There are doubts about the near-term commercial viability and profitability of such national broadband networks based on ubiquitous – or near universal – fibre optic to households. Hence the surprising situation whereby countries which had declared the market would deliver communications and media services – through privatization and liberalization policies of the 1980s and 1990s – are now turning to their governments to directly invest, underwrite or otherwise enable the next-generation broadband networks.

As such networks eventuate – and there are clear signs that they will, with a number of governments committing to, or already commencing plans, to create widespread fast broadband networks (Berkman Center for Internet and Society, 2010) – they are set to have profound implications for media already in transition. What is obvious is that the effect of the internet upon other media forms will deepen. Television, for instance, can be broadcast in a much more pervasive, higher-quality, greatly more controllable and commodified way, over these broadband networks than presently. The much vaunted project of digital broadcasting has already been interwoven with – even dictated to – by user-driven internet developments such as podcasting, programme-downloading (whether BitTorrent or 'catch-up' television) or broadcasting of television and radio via the internet. If next-generation broadband networks eventuate, taking over from telecommunications networks as the universal communications infrastructure, then there will be a pipe, as it were, that goes into most, if not all, households in a nation. When television can be broadcast – piped down – the next-generation broadband networks, and finally the visions of video-on-demand and interactivity that date back to at least the 1990s can be realized (Van Tassel, 2001), why would broadcasters ultimately bother to maintain a distinct infrastructure of broadcasting towers, transmitters and the expensive software and hardware that this requires? In this scenario, IP television moves from being a niche product, captive to the exigencies and unreliable quality of much domestic internet connection and service, to *the* dominant and pervasive mode of television broadcasting. At which point, existing broadcasters may well decide to abandon the existing transmission infrastructure in favour of internet television (Alcatel-Lucent, 2009). Of course, this scenario is fraught – not least because the actual endeavour of constructing these next-generation networks is a minefield of technical and commercial difficulties and battles. Thus hybrid media platforms with a mess of underlying infrastructures are likely to be with us for a long time to come. Nonetheless the scale and scope of the challenge of internet to television (Owen, 1999), and the importance of the clashes, and technical and social innovations at the tense collision of these tectonic plates cannot now be underestimated.

Generation User and Personal Media

Already we have encountered the figure of the user, resplendent at the heart of new technologies – if not installed at the heart of social media. Social media is but one of many instances in which contemporary media, and the discourses that play an important role in constructing them, rely upon users and consumers of media.

Over three decades' research, especially audience studies, has shown the active role that those reading, listening to, viewing and discussing media play in completing or indeed play in creating the media themselves. The neglect of the audience is well on the way to being addressed, but in new technologies particularly, we have new aspects and attributes of how audiences form, act and relate to media. It is evident that audiences *interact* with media, in the sense that someone interacts with a computer programme, or games. The role of choice is much heightened with the advent of new technologies. In the case of television, it has been dramatically played out through substantial portions of audiences being unwilling to wait for programmes to be screened, or even to use the record-and-replay technologies created and designated by broadcasters (timid versions of a fully fledged TiVo, discussed in Chapter 4), and so download, upload and share programmes with other audiences members around the world.

Audiences have not only moved centre-stage in how we understand media, they are at the heart of its very creation and reproduction (Nightingale, 2011). This can perhaps be most clearly grasped in the example of content-sharing communities, such as YouTube (Burgess and Green, 2009). Certainly there are 'channels' on YouTube provided by various professional media producers and broadcasters, and a range of other media institutions. However, we find organizations that would previously have turned to media companies to produce and distribute documentaries, videos, educational or promotional material on their behalf doing so themselves instead. Further, we find all sorts of other much more informal groups or indeed a teeming multitude of individuals making and uploading videos to video-sharing sites. Such material no longer has to conform to the requirements or canons of mainstream media gatekeepers, or even that of community, civic or public broadcasters. Any single individual with sufficient digital literacy and equipment – which poses problems for the majority of the world's population – can participate in these new kinds of public spheres (Hartley, 2009). This phenomenon is often referred to as 'pro-am' (Leadbeater, 2004), the distinctive new ways in which media professionals and workers and amateur media consumers-cum-producers – what Axel Bruns terms 'produsers' (Bruns, 2008) – are now closely linked across the range of media, including mainstream outlets. Newspapers, for instance, solicit and at times rely upon amateur photographers to email in videos or pictures of breaking news.

In many ways, media have become personal (Baym, 2010; Ganley, 1992; Hawk, Rieder and Oviedo, 2008). Previously a television programme would be broadcast to an abstract audience, who may be known or researched through surveys or people meters (for the notorious activity of gauging rates, not least to assuage the concerns of advertisers), fan magazines or ethnographies. With the advent of subscription television, and especially the vast crypt of personal and private information available through the internet, the personal viewing and other media habits, and preferences of audience members can be known at a very intimate level. Thus companies have invested heavily in ways of knowing not just demographic groups, regional areas, particular markets or households, but particular individuals. Just as politicians now construct databases to gather and update information on every voter on an electoral roll, so too do media companies collect or 'mine' data that help personalize services. The expectation of personalization is widespread among consumers of media too, and is catered for by media companies using new technologies. One of the great masters of this dark art is Google, with its 'iGoogle' default webpage, allowing users to customize the look, feel and resident applications (or widgets) on their home page. Trends in computing and data networking underpin this turn to personal media. There is an increasing tendency for individuals to own particular devices – whether 'personal' computers', laptops, game devices or mobile phones. Then there is the move towards 'software as a service' and 'cloud computing', where a user no longer needs to purchase programs, which have to be installed and stored on their own computer. Rather one logs in, and the programs and files can be accessed across the network.

Seeking to capture the ramifications of these digital cultures, theorists have term these 'participatory cultures' (Burgess and Green, 2009; Jenkins, 2006), or 'do-it-yourself cultures'. The idea is that users are now able to participate in media in extensive ways that were previously much more difficult to do (Organization for Economic Cooperation and Development, 2007). A number of scholars have pointed out that such notions and structures of participation have long histories and operate in quite specific contexts (Carpentier and De Cleen, 2008). A debate is underway also regarding the nature and politics of such participation

(Siegel, 2007) – not surprisingly given that participation is a key concern across different areas, not least social and political life. What participation means remains contested. What norms and values underlie participation and how such visions of participation are to be secured are matters for debate. Participation in digital cultures raises new questions for what we see as the rights and obligations of users (Goggin and Hjorth, 2009). In addition, there are the questions of what significance participation in these new media settings holds for general understanding of participation. It is worthwhile pausing, therefore, to think hard about participation as it is designated as a key axis of new technologies and the media. This is especially important when it comes to the vogue – or should I say 'vague' – topic of Web 2.0.

For many, the defining aspect of new technologies and the media today is something called 'Web 2.0'. Web 2.0 is a portmanteau concept, stretching even wider than its overlapping counterpart social media. Famously popularized by technology writer, publisher and marketing entrepreneur Tim O'Reilly through his 'Web 2.0' conferences from 2004 onwards (O'Reilly, 2005), the term connotes a new era in media based on internet developments of user participation and content generation, interactivity and sharing. Along with Web 2.0, argues *Wired* magazine editor Chris Anderson, comes a new aspect of economics called the 'long tail' (Anderson, 2006). Because of the various developments articulating through the user, profits can be made through focusing on niche, marginal products and services – rather than the very popular services that statistically are the most used (the long tail referring to the last few percent of consumers that are usually thought to take too many extra resources to serve).

By 2009 the term web 2.0 was widely used, but often lacking any precision. The obvious problem with Web 2.0 is that it conflates quite different attributes of internet technology, some having a relatively long lineage – and suggests that the internet after some rather unspecified classic phase of Web 1.0 has fundamentally changed. As such it is best regarded as a loose bid for invoking a *Zeitgeist* – or at best a particular ideology, or moment – rather than an especially useful analytic tool (Allen, 2008, 2009; Scholz, 2008). The critique of Web 2.0 is valuable when we return to consideration of what role the user plays, and is invoked to play, in this historical moment.

Much of the discourse on the user emphasizes the constructive and creative role of this now central figure (Haddon, Mante, Sapio *et al.*, 2005). From quite different standpoints, there is a loose consensus that technologies, and the economies in which they are embedded, need their users in more radical, fundamental ways than they did previously (Von Hippel, 2005). The rise of innovation as concept also expands to become a governing logic of media industries. This is most clearly glimpsed in the notion of 'creative industries' (Flew, 2011; Hartley, 2005), where creativity and innovation broaden beyond their traditional setting in the arts, culture, science and technology to become pervasive features of not only media but manufacturing and service economies. At a minimum, users are equal partners in 'co-construction' of technologies (Oudshoorn and Pinch, 2003) – and participatory cultures reshaping media are a case in point (Greif, Hjorth, Lasén and Lobet-Maris, 2011).

Yet the freedom of users to enter into such arrangements of continuous or at least regular, and widespread, innovation, content-generation, and so on is a moot point. It is something of an exhausting and enervating spectacle: the always-on media technologies such as broadband internet need to be matched by the ever-consuming, contributing, tweeting, blogging, filesharing and content-devising masses. At times there seems to be very little difference between urging users to participate in new technology, and a new system compelling them to do so. Thus many have now critiqued the relations of labour and leisure in this new economy and its virtual, online worlds, where the value contributed by users and consumers is so necessary – and often so taken for granted, if not outright alienated by the digital media corporations in the ascendancy (Deuze, 2007; Mosco and McKercher, 2008; Ross, 2009).

Mobile and Wireless Networks

From audiences and users, let us turn to mobile and wireless networks – an important part of the technologies that underpin these media developments and discourses. As I have noted, evolving standards, equipment and networks of press and broadcasting are contending with the 'creative destruction' (Schumpeter, 1943) of internet innovation. Coupled with the internet is the influence of mobile and wireless technologies and networks on the media. Offered commercially in Japan and the US in the late 1970s, the cellular mobile phone surpassed the figure of 5 billion subscribers worldwide during 2010. The 'cell phone' – as it is known especially in the US, though it has many other names in other languages and countries – is based on a method of dividing radio spectrum into 'cells' of between 1–100 kilometres radius, allowing efficient transmission of signals to phones within a given cell, then transfer of signals across cells. As the analogue phone developed and its bulk and price dropped during the 1980s, it was first popular as a way for users to make and receive telephone calls. This untethering of the telephone from its fixed place in homes, workplaces or phone booths initially caused wonderment and consternation that still resonate today. Telephone communication had long been important in the practice of journalism, as a crucial way for reporters to maintain links with sources, research stories, conduct interviews or file stories. To some extent, the contacts list on a mobile phone supplanted the prized address book or contacts list of working journalists. However, it was social and technical innovations in mobile technology and their uses in the 1990s that laid the foundations for their subsequent importance.

The 'second-generation' (2G) cellular mobile networks deployed from the early 1990s were digital. 2G handsets and networks supported many more applications than their 1G forebears, affording much greater computer power, computing operating systems and applications. The standards that underpinned 2G mobiles were predicated on mobiles as fully fledged data and multimedia technologies – especially when 2G evolved into 3G (third generation). With 2G mobiles, various kinds of applications flourished, from mobile games and music through mobile internet to one of the most popular features of all – mobile images. Ironically, perhaps the most popular and defining application of mobile-phone culture in this classic period in the 1990s was text messaging, defined by the rise of the short-message-service (SMS). However the story is told, SMS was an unexpected boon.

Written into the standards underlying 2G, it was envisaged as a rudimentary text-communication system thought to be helpful for network maintenance and troubleshooting. Instead SMS was adopted in all sorts of unexpected ways by many different groups of users around the world. Early on it was identified with youth culture, especially as it surfaced as a social-networking tool for young Finns. In other countries young people also embraced and refashioned SMS, leading to public discussion of the various ills thought to be associated with it. These social anxieties – many of them full-blown 'moral panics', as sociology and cultural theory would classify these – included the dumbing down of culture through the deterioration of knowledge of grammar and linguistic standards, the solipsistic, inward-looking lives and friendship cultures of young texters, and the threats to vulnerable children and young people from a device that allows communication without parental awareness or monitoring. As it spread, SMS was used by other age groups, demographics and kinds of communities. Deaf people were avid users of SMS, as a portable text technology superior to text tele-phones (teletypewriter devices) popularly used since the 1980s. Everyday use of SMS became widespread because it offered a discreet, relatively ubiquitous mode of communication, which, unlike the intru-sion of the telephone, allowed people to text while in meetings, lectures, the bed or bathroom, while walking or driving (unsafely, of course), in company, while dining, away from home or in the same room.

The popularity of SMS thrilled the mobile-phone companies, who swooned over this lucrative new source of products and services. It was also music to the ears of a new clutch of companies that designed and sold products and services based on SMS, directly to users or as part of the mobile 'portals' or 'premium' mobile services offered by carriers and providers. SMS broadened from text alerts, stockmarket updates, news, text chats to play a handy role in the development of mobile commerce ('m-commerce') and indeed electronic commerce ('e-commerce') because it was a more secure transaction and payment channel that was available via the internet (even with the use of encryption technologies and trusted payment systems).

SMS was the first example of a distinctly new form of 'mobile media'. It might still sound odd to regard a telephone-based technology such as the mobile phone as a media form. Yet this is precisely what mobiles are now recognized as. In the case of SMS, we have an application that vaulted the mobile phone well beyond anything we might expect from the accepted communicative practices, cultural significance and social functions of the telephone in its heyday from, say, 1920 to the early 1990s, when the telephone achieved something approximating 'univer-sal' coverage in wealthy countries. Nor was SMS merely a communi-cation device, allowing interpersonal, group or organization communication – far-reaching though this role was. For instance, SMS became identified with dissent, protest and activism, with commenta-tors evincing fascination for the distinct ways in which SMS could assemble and organize demonstrations, movements and social and political action. Especially as it developed from the early 2000s onwards, SMS assumed media-like attributes: it disseminated informa-tion, facilitated expression, allowed users to participate in social and political action, and claim membership in 'imagined communities' and became a significant technology in defining and constituting culture.

If my argument holds, this proto-media emergence of SMS, as a pivotal part of mobiles, becomes much more evident in the great diffu-sion of mobile phones through developing countries and emerging markets. This face of SMS as media is captured in Jonathan Donner's evocative phrase 'mobile media on low-cost handsets' to describe the small- and informal-business use of text messaging in India (Donner, 2009). As well as providing access to market information for fishermen, a celebrated case from Kerala, India (Abraham, 2007), a tool for customers to purchase items, SMS supports provision of health information, polling, social support and community development. These are uses that expand our customary ideas of media, which are amply evident in SMS too, notably the use of messaging in news gathering and reporting in a number of projects in Africa (Bruijn, Nyamnjoh and Brinkman, 2009; Ekine, 2010).

Hot on the heels of SMS followed MMS (multimedia messaging) allowing users to send and receive photos or videos. The camera phone was first developed in Japan in 2001, and rapidly became standard in new mobile phones. Like SMS, MMS was a send-and-forward technology by which users could take a photo or short video clip on their phone and message it to a friend. Interestingly MMS did not receive the same acclaim across user groups that SMS did – a slower development path not assisted by difficulties with compatibility across platforms and handsets. Faced with the obstacles of usability, bandwidth and cost for sending images via MMS, more often than not users instead uploaded photos and videos to the internet. Whether via plugging the phone into a computer via a cable, sending the image via Bluetooth, through the WiFi mode of a mobile phone, copying from a memory card or through mobile email, users could quickly transfer an image to a computer and use the relatively cheaper, faster and more versatile capabilities of the internet to distribute their photographic bounty. The teeming population of mobile users now came into its own. The vast reservoir of camera-phone images could be harnessed in the new forms of media, especially key to the production of video for sites like YouTube.

The importance of this mobile–internet link for media can be observed in at least two instances. It provided new modes of reporting and distribution for material that would otherwise not find its way into national media, or even international media, and that was of considerable significance. The case of coverage of dissent in Burma in 2008 is testament to this. Mainstream media in Burma is very highly restricted, and even new media based on internet or mobiles are subject to control and penalties. Yet because of the common ownership of mobiles, even at the relatively low rates in Burma, it is as difficult to control all uses of all mobiles – as it is to intercept and interdict all uses of the internet. Once content can be uploaded to the internet, it can be viewed immediately and become part of news distribution, reception, debate, and media and public relations efforts by official sources, all in a very fast feedback loop.

As well as mobile-internet media ecologies playing a strategically important part in the traditional Fourth Estate of media, we can observe signs of a shift in what is understood by the term, media. People are able to use mobile devices to produce text, images, sounds and other forms of media for consumption by small and large groups. The gatekeepers – to take the classic notion of those controlling media such as journalists, editors, advertisers, media company owners, managers and proprietors – have transmogrified into 'gatewatchers', as Axel Bruns puts it (Bruns, 2005). What counts as news really now can be in the eye or mouse-click of the beholder. Everyday news of interest to particular individuals and the groupuscles or micro-audiences they belong to – let's call this 'little news' – blurs into the designation, production and dissemination of what is considered 'the news' and the news agenda that shape this 'big' or 'major' news. Blogs or Twitter feeds convey a sense of this, where the quotidian, texture and grain of an individual's life often sits alongside their posts or Tweets about a media event of lasting international significance (Crawford, 2009). Of course, newspapers have also been composed of a range of different sections – from international or national news, through sports and business pages, social commentary, editorials and op-eds to quizzes, crosswords and gossip columns. Mobiles are another distinct and pervasive component of how media is being reconceived to rework these categories, their relationships to each other and the hierarchy of values and economy of attention in which they operate.

Before we conclude our conspectus of mobiles in the field of new technologies and the media, it is important to note several further advances. The third generation of mobile phones (3G) introduced from the early 2000s, while slow to develop, eventually established a platform for the mobile to explicitly confront media. Mobile television, as we shall see, explicitly begins as a project of reimagining television for mobiles – broadcasting television signals directly to mobile phones. The idea of mobiles as a 'fourth screen', sitting alongside television, cinema and computers, captures the imagination of movie- and video-makers, and the audiovisual industries in which they sit. It is possible to make a movie with a mobile phone. It is also possible to watch a video, short film or feature-length title on a handset (computing power, screen size and resolution, and network capacity permitting). While these initial imaginings of mobile media entrepreneurs did not exactly go to plan, at the very least mobiles are now firmly embedded in our contemporary notion of the media environment (Goggin, 2011b). Media producers and audiences are experimenting with what works, and what does not, for mobiles, as part of the cross-platform conception of media. Content is produced, reconfigured and 'repurposed' (as the maladroit verb has it) for mobile devices, as it is for radio, television, newspapers – or even cinema, DVD, advertising and games. There are new relationships of dependency of media forms that integrally involve mobiles. A radio programme may carry an abridged interview, that can be viewed on the web, podcast to a digital music player or mobile, commented on via internet or mobile, with links or excerpts sent from all manner of devices.

Clearly mobiles are a key actor in the adaptations of media that are now widely used, from SMS, camera phones or games, to mobile television and movies. In most of these, the seam of realignment and innovation between mobiles and the internet recurs as dynamic and important. This is evident in the final aspect of mobile media I wish to note: smartphones. Smartphones are advanced phones with computing and multimedia capacities well beyond those customary for 2G phones and even many 3Gs (at least in their first decade). Though smartphones were available and promoted as cutting edge and very modern from at least 2005 onwards, it was the rapturous reception of Apple's iPhone that saw a new sense of mobile-oriented media emerge. With design and usability advances – offering new features and affordances, while eclipsing or losing formerly cherished capabilities – the iPhone and other smartphones such as those using Google's Android operating system opened up new possibilities for media. The second coming of smartphones builds upon, and develops, the fertile seam between mobiles and the internet, something also thematized in visions of fourth-generation (4G) technology that combines wireless and mobile networks.

Conclusion

This chapter has offered a necessarily brief overview of new technologies key to the media, centring on digital networks – especially the internet and mobiles. We can apply the ideas from the first part of the chapter, regarding the importance of taking a critical stance, to trouble the clear lines and progressive vision of the development of such networks. As emphasized in the various theories of technology I pointed to, it turns out that technologies do not come to us fully formed, like the goddess Minerva from the head of Jove. Like rhizomes rather than seeds, technologies sprout, find nourishment and support, and shoot in unexpected directions.

The great march of mobile technologies through numbered generations – 1, 2, 3, 4 and so on – is especially simplistic. The infrastructures themselves are agglomerations of particular choices and accidents of technology implementation. The headline statistic about the number of phones in the developing world today appears marvellous and miraculous. The investments and economic benefits involved wholesale reworking of national economic structures. Yet when we scratch the surface we find: technologies that people do not use, or barely use or use for other purposes; people owning mobile phones, but living in villages where there is no electricity – so they cannot charge them easily; users who cannot afford to use the phone much for calling, texting or other functions, so instead Bluetooth files to their phones, and show each other photos on the screen.

If we can take our societies' stories about new technologies with a grain of salt, then we will be well disposed to be capable of attending carefully to unravelling the threads of how these artefacts, systems, feelings, ideas, economies and other things that comprise technology, are interwoven in the warp and weft of the media – a theme central to the chapters that follow.

3 What's News: The Press and New Technologies

> The technology once deemed to be a possible savior has emerged as a tool of the very interests at the root of the crisis. The boom and bust cycle of the new economy did not produce a democratized media with decentralized news production and a more informed polity. Rather, it resulted in a hard-nosed set of business strategies that is rapidly handing even greater control over public information to an ever-decreasing number of media corporations
>
> Ben Scott (Scott, 2005, pp. 121–2)

> WikiLeaks Defence Cables – Read It First in the *Herald*.
> (*Sydney Morning Herald* advertising placard, December 2010)

In the defining moments of societies, at the decision-making junctures for democracies, during periods of war, disaster and national mourning, we are reminded of the enduring importance of the press. The press – the newspaper industry – is deeply embedded in the routines, the high points and lows, the crises and interruptions, the shifts and continuities of public and private lives. The nature and function of the media has changed greatly: simply put, we have more media, new kinds of media and different relationships with them, and their role in our daily lives often feels much greater.

Yet the press is resilient and continues to be invested with great significance, despite recurrent predictions of its demise. The press has been the long-standing media of several centuries, regarded by many as definitive. For historical and other reasons, news, public life and politics remain at the heart of the press in a way that they do not for the electronic media. The newspaper industry has changed greatly in recent times, with metamorphoses that go to the heart of what we understand as news and entertainment, and the relationship between the press, truth, reality and narrative. New technology is deeply entwined in these media transformations.

In particular, the internet has greatly altered the dynamics of newspapers and news. Journalists are now reliant on the internet for much of their information. Newspapers themselves have embraced – often unwillingly – the internet for distribution, not least because the traditional print-based titles face intense competition from the multitude of sources of news available via the internet. Thus newspapers have incorporated the internet into their operations. Websites, social media, online and mobile news are highly visible and significant elements of contemporary newspapers.

Most dramatically, having reached an accommodation of sorts with the internet, newspapers are now at a crossroads. Having survived two decades of the web, and four decades of the internet itself, the demise of newspapers – in some countries at least – is at hand. As well as sales of papers, advertising has been an indispensable source of revenue and profits. In the 2000s especially, we have seen a widespread migration of advertising to the internet. The lucrative area of classified ads – for goods and services, such as cars, accommodation and real estate, and job vacancies – moved quickly to the internet, while other advertising followed. New forms of advertising distinctive to the internet were created, underpinned by the centrality of search engines. Thus the old business model of newspapers is dissolving fast, as sales of and subscriptions to newspapers struggle, and advertising revenues plummet. Newspapers have not enjoyed much success selling their content via the internet, but now proprietors are hoping paywalls and apps will finally persuade readers to pay for digital news.

Against this backdrop, this chapter aims to elucidate the operation of technologies when it comes to the press. To do so, I will focus upon only one aspect of the press – news. The press does many other things than report, frame, construct and communicate news. However, news, and all it signifies, is regarded as vitally important for the operation of society – and especially for the normative foundations of democracies. News is the very stuff of culture (Allan, 2004; Bird, 2010; McNair, 2006). Over time, the press has been shot through by particular technologies, notably those of the printing press, paper, telegraph, telephone, shorthand and the tape recorder – all of which have affected news framing, gathering, reporting, transmission and reception. The change that new technologies have brought to newspapers is a key area of enquiry and debate among those concerned about the media.

Thus, in this chapter, I focus on the networked digital technologies of the internet, exploring their role in contemporary press transformations and challenges. The chapter opens by tracing the development of online news, with its antecedents in forms such as videotexts and early internet news. I turn to discussion of the broadening of news into online media from the mid-1990s to early 2000s, when newspapers were challenged and fundamentally reshaped by a set of developments centring on users, open systems and new media cultures. After this, I look at how the nature of news gathering, journalism and media work has changed with new technologies, with case studies of new kinds of news agencies, as well as the controversial WikiLeaks website. Finally, the chapter closes with an analysis of mobile news, especially centring on the strategies of Rupert Murdoch's News Corporation in relation to hand-held devices such as e-readers, smartphones, tablets and iPads.

The Long History of Online News

In the face of promises, exaggerations and boons proffered by promoters of online (and mobile) news, it is helpful to remind ourselves of the relevant histories of the new form. There are various ways to approach the history of online news, but I wish to present four strands here: the rise of computer-based, network-distributed information services and databases; the excitement surrounding teletext and videotext – that is, the text-based services forming part of new television services in the 1970s and 1980s, as well as telecommunications interactivity as an adjunct to broadcasting; the early online cultures of particular networking systems, offered as public initiatives (the French Minitel or British Prestel system) or private, proprietary systems (America Online); and the emergent kinds of collaborative, user-driven news communities on bulletin-board systems and internet cultures (such as newsgroups).

The beginnings of online information services stretch back at least to the early 1960s (Bourne and Hahn, 2003). With the development of computing, it became possible to store and retrieve increasingly large amounts of information – especially with the advent of sophisticated database programs. Computers could also be connected to telecommunications and data networks, so that information could be distributed around nodes of the network, and accessed by remote users. Students and academics are now very familiar with online information services because much of academic literature is discovered and retrieved through databases and the aggregation of academic journal content by publishers. Books are also increasingly distributed in electronic forms, again with purpose-built links to databases and catalogues.

In broadcasting, text services were precursors of what we now regard as online information and news services. Broadcast television signals had space in their transmission that were not utilized as fully as they might be. This space could allow text to be carried in gaps between important parts of television content. Accordingly, two new kinds of services were developed to supplement the news and information available in televisual formats: teletext and videotext. These new television services were thought to be, in the evocative words of a leading study, an 'emerging economy of words' (Jouët, Flichy and Beaud, 1991). News services were thought be especially promising (Organization for Economic Cooperation and Development, 1998; Winsbury, 1979; Woolfe, 1980). Teletext and videotext – as types of what the French call *télématique* (telematics) – were thought to hold great promise for fleshing out the 'information society' (Aldrich, 1982; Mayne, 1982), though ultimately the services were deemed to have 'failed' (Graziplene, 2000).

Like online information services, teletext and videotext represented an explicit attempt by large corporations and entrepreneurs to create new services and markets in news. The videotext experiment involved the creation of networks of terminals by which users could access online services, information and news. One of the most popular initiatives was the French Minitel service, established by the government posts, telegraph and telephone administration in the early 1980s. Used by millions of French citizens, it provided information, booking, a database and new services (Marchand, 1987; OECD, 1998). Another such undertaking was the British Prestel (or Viewdata) system, offered by the Post Office in that country (Fedida and Malik, 1979; Winsbury, 1981). In the US, Prodigy was an early, popular parallel service, followed by data and networking services offered by other big pre-internet companies such as America Online (AOL) and CompuServe (Aspray and Ceruzzi, 2008).

As we can already see, there are overlaps among these different pioneers of online news. Each approach to the technology accented a particular facet of services, created distinctive features, design and applications – or 'affordances', as James J. Gibson termed them (Gibson, 1977). Each distinct technology allowed – or required – people to imagine online media and news along specific lines. The rise of the internet relied upon, and interacted with, these other kinds of technologies and services. As it broadened its base of users, however, the internet can be seen – even relatively early on – to suggest other ways of approaching new technologies and the media.

Electronic mail proved an important way for people to share news informally. Software was devised called listservers ('listserv') that allowed broadcast of messages to lists of email addresses so that news and information could be quickly distributed from one user to many.

Another technology that proved influential in early internet cultures was the newsgroup software. Collected through something called Usenet, newsgroups allowed people with an interest in specialized topics to form groups. Although 'news' did not at first signify the traditional form of media, newsgroups were influential as a way to open debate, exchange information, files and images – especially concerning alternative, minority and less frequently ventilated topics in the mainstream press. For internet pioneers, newsgroups even created new forms of citizenship, something Michael and Ronda Hauben, for instance, celebrated as 'netizens' (Hauben and Hauben, 1997). These early developments in internet cultures were neither widely noticed by, nor did they immediately influence developments in the press. However, they did prefigure important facets of the social, online and mobile media of the present time – so we will take up these themes a little later on. Where the internet garnered a very large following very quickly indeed was the World Wide Web.

Invented in the late 1980s, and made available with a free browser in the early 1990s, the web coincided with – and greatly accelerated – the mass, popular take-up of the internet. The protocols of the web, and the form of the website, brought together in an easy form the dispersed applications of the internet. Through a web browser, one could use email, chat and messaging; uploading and distribution of files and images suddenly became much easier; and so too did identifying a location on the internet (through the web known as Uniform Resource Locator, or URL). It was easy for individuals to design their own websites, so webcultures flourished with a wave of do-it-yourself experimentation, lending support not only to existing mainstream culture, but also subcultures and minority cultures (Consalvo and Paasonen, 2002; Gauntlett and Horsley, 2004; Wellman and Haythornwaite, 2002).

The appeal and facility of the website were not lost on the press. Amateurs, often very skilled and knowledgeable, were bypassing established media, entertainment and information providers to make criticism, commentary, opinion and news available on their own websites – which could be easily maintained, publicized and linked to other websites or internet resources. Seeing an opportunity, and fearing the competition, well-established newspapers began to develop their own websites. So began in earnest newspapers' engagement with the internet as a vital channel of distribution of their content. Through this sometimes reluctant and uncomprehending embrace of internet came experimentation about where the internet fitted into the press. Or, rather, where the press was to take its place in the media worlds in which the internet dominated. In his examination of the first decade of online journalism on the web, Mark Deuze discerns four types of online journalism, which vary according to their concentration towards editorial content or public participation: mainstream news sites; index and category sites; meta and comment sites; share and discussion sites (Deuze, 2003).

Many of the early newspaper websites did not attract readerships in the manner those establishing them had envisaged. However, certainly by the late 1990s newspaper websites were widely used. While only a minor proportion overall relied solely on websites to 'read' a newspaper, many others did wish to be able to consult a website, with a known, trusted newspaper title (or 'brand') in order to find breaking news, content where they were away from traditional outlets (for example, travelling, residing abroad), or yesterday's or archived news. New habits of newspaper reading became common – for instance, being able to easily see other related stories previously filed or printed, through links. Previously separate arms of the same press organization now potentially made their content available via the internet: 'traditionally distinct segments of the news industry itself, print (dailies, weeklies, and magazines) and broadcast (networks, cable, and radio), found themselves competing head to head for users and advertisers' (Scott, 2005, p. 95).

So newspapers slowly and uncomfortably accustomed themselves to the new technological medium ('platform') of the internet. Their ability to make such a change is captured in Deuze's still apposite observation that:

> a news medium considering or implementing new strategies has to enable its organization to reflexively address the existing journalistic culture and rethink its location on the continuum between content and connectivity. If not, it cannot be expected to fully grasp the consequences of these changes – and thus it cannot be expected to succeed.
>
> (Deuze, 2003, p. 220)

The central difficulty that presented itself toward the end of the web's first decade, however, lay in the economical and commercial basis of the new, networked press. How could newspapers make the internet pay? Newspapers tried to control distribution of their content on websites, by requesting a subscription fee, or per-view payment. Only in rare cases have consumers been willing to pay for newspapers online. Exceptions include much-sought-after financial press (the *Financial Times*, for instance), subscription-only internet newspapers (the Australian political commentary title *Crikey.com*, or advertising-supported press (such as the *Craigslist* in the US, which mostly supports free local advertising, but has some paid ads such as job ads in various cities). The models used have often been 'freemium', offering consumers some free content – then requiring payment or subscription for extra, 'premium' content. As we shall see, the web would complete its second decade before any general consumer acceptance of paying for newspapers online emerged.

General economic confidence in the internet's prospect for business peaked with the speculation associated with the dot.com boom of the late 1990s, quickly followed by the terrible bust that saw trillions of dollars shed from the value of internet stocks, but also, though rather overlooked, from telecommunications ('telco') shares. Investor confidence in the internet was slow to recover following its 'first recession' (Lovink, 2003) and the press played a leading part in media industries' efforts to make the technology safe for business. This domestication of the internet by established, mainstream media was about to become all the more difficult. The internet, its developers and users had a great capacity to generate even more unexpected innovations – with dramatic implications for how media is understood and financed.

Websites, Cultures and Blogs

If the press managed an uneasy accommodation of sorts with the internet, the technology's intense growth and innovation was about to make things a whole lot rougher. Less than a decade after the arrival of the website came the blog. Based on the underlying technology and cultures of the web, the blog brought new genres into play (or, rather, activated older genres).

Blogs allowed electronic diaries to be kept in the public setting of the web. Blogs also breathed life into the journal – a form similar to a diary (keeping an account and record of one's personal life) that also engages with literary, political and social issues. After a short period of experimentation, purpose-built software for blogs became readily available, and it provided an easy way for those interested, motivated and capable of doing so, to take up blogging. A defining feature of blogs is regular entries, usually short in length – 'blog posts'. The other defining feature is commentary from those reading the blog – which immediately allowed conversations (productive or vituperative, or both) to be made. Blogging software – such as LiveJournal or Movable Type – created particular features and applications to support these and other aspects of blogging cultures.

While blogs offered a new kind of informal media for individuals and groups to record and represent their lives and the things which interested them, the openness of the platform, the interconnected nature of blogs – captured in the word 'blogosphere' – and the velocity and impact of some blogs in the wider internet, saw blogs become a significant media form in their own right. In many countries, consumers went to blogs for their news and other media, rather than the press. In the US, the *Drudge Report* achieved notoriety because founder Matt Drudge was prepared to break stories that other newspaper, television and radio outlets were chary of doing because they did not meet the standards of evidence customarily applied. Blogs were able to break news sometimes even more quickly than the twenty-four-hour news channels that had emerged from the early 1990s – and so audiences turned to them in times of crisis. Blogs often provided additional perspectives and information. They introduced new ways of breaking and consuming news, and indeed altered the nature of the 'news cycle', and the norms and ethics of reporting.

The role of interactivity (comment especially) and interlinking among bloggers led to a new orientation among readers (represented in the notion of the 'blogosphere'), with heightened expectations about how the press should function. For their part, newspapers responded by incorporating blogs, and other online media forms, into their operations. Blogs also allowed readers to comment on stories. Reader feedback had been commonly used in websites and message boards, often used on media program or corporation websites, to add response to and interaction with audiences. Blogs took such limited interaction further, and put it at the heart of the form; at least until bloggers were overwhelmed – or shouted down – by the irruption of irrationality, with sheer abuse often common (Lovink, 2008).

Blogs as a form veered uneasily between resembling a fantastic conversation, on the one hand, and a nasty slanging match, on the other – but certainly became quickly established as a major force in media and political culture. Blogs were embraced early on by conservative groups and the right (especially in the US), as a reaction against the perceived dominance of left-liberal media. Other political groups across the spectrum also turned to blogs to express their views, making the new technologies an important site for oppositional struggle (Kahn and Kellner, 2008). So-called 'A'-list bloggers were media commentators or personalities who developed a strong following and profile. New bloggers – especially young media aspirants – often came to notice, then gained media fame and even considerable power through blogging, then parlayed this into wider media reach. Experienced media pundits were also able to use blogs as a platform for their writing, hence the phenomenon of established newspaper and magazine columnists maintaining a blog as an integral part of their work. Such rich interactions between journalism and blogging are captured in the concept 'j-blogging', which refers to blogs maintained by journalists. J-blogging can encompass the kind of 'official' blogs of journalists clearly paid for and forming part of their existing press role and title. Or j-blogging can also indicate the skilful manoeuvres of journalists who maintain a blog to seek the independence of comment that their day job at a mainstream media outlet may not allow (Yu, 2010).

Certainly, blogs have established themselves as a key platform in the media (Rettberg, 2008; Tremayne, 2007). Indeed, there is considerable interdependence in a number of respects between blogs and newspapers. There are important qualifications to be made about the power of blogs as news media. Blogs can certainly affect the agenda setting of newspapers. In addition, blogs – and social media – often have their own distinctive agenda, compared to newspapers, something that continues to be the subject of research and debate, as tracked, for instance, by the regular Pew Centre studies of news in the US (Pew Centre, 2011). However, a great many blogs rely heavily on newspapers for initial information – what has been called the 'source cycle' (Lecesse, 2009; Messner and Distaso, 2008). This is reminiscent of the way that reportage and analysis in morning newspapers leads to further coverage and discussion during the day on radio and television.

There is a great sprawling mass of blogs – from the bulk that suffer the fate of 'zero comment' (or at least tiny audiences) through niche or specialized blogs to the many blogs that are read by very large or very significant audiences. Mapping the blogosphere, and measuring and evaluating its impact upon media economies and systems have proven difficult. There are metrics that allow traffic, use and linking of blogs to other blogs, and other parts of the internet, to be gauged. However, researchers are still striving to provide us with grounded conceptualizations of the exact ways in which various blogospheres work and, especially, what their connections are to other media and public spheres (Bruns, 2008; Meyers, 2010; Tremayne, 2007). For example, there have been various studies of the US blogosphere and its political systems and cultures – as the rise of blogging directly fed into US mainstream politics and elections in a spectacular fashion (Perlmutter, 2008). There is a burgeoning body of work on international blogging (Loewenstein, 2008; Russell and Echchaibi, 2009). We need such research and debate on blogs to establish where they fit into the nexus between media and politics. A central difficulty here is that both of these governing concepts – media and politics – have each changed profoundly. Nonetheless our accounts of how power works, how societies are structured, and what prospects for democracy are (and how democracy can be nurtured or sustained), all rely upon assumptions about the media. When new technologies make their entrance – as blogs have so colourfully and pervasively done – then the debate about their implications is a high-stakes affair, because media now underpins politics, and political arrangements, so directly and decisively.

Our News Agencies

It is fair to regard the web – and the amazing reliance societies began to place upon it – as functioning as a circulating and gathering medium for other internet technologies, such as blogs and social media. To understand fully how this unfolds, we need to appreciate the histories of the decentralized, collaborative news gathering which achieves momentum and new expression with the internet. From at least the mid-1990s onwards, the internet became widely used to allow new kinds of organizations to gather, collate, arrange and make available news. This is most strikingly evident in a number of experiments with open news. Open news is the idea that the process of news gathering, making, redacting and distribution can be rendered transparent, and undertaken by ordinary citizens, not just media professionals and their organizations (Bruns, 2005). Hence open news can be created from any number of sources, from individuals or groups voluntarily contributing, filtering and editing material.

In various countries in the late 1990s, progressive social groups established 'Independent Media Centres', spawning the Indymedia movement. Indymedia websites were established, and linked to each other, using internet technology as well as design and adaptation applications. Activists, volunteers and interested individuals could upload news to an Indymedia website, which could then be easily disseminated, through RSS (Really Simple Syndication) feeds, email lists, web links) (Meikle, 2002). The presentation and circulation of news through Indymedia's outlets did offer an important alternative perspective in a period before blogs and the growth of news portals.

Indymedia also played an important role in the anti-globalization movements that were salient in the late 1990s and continued to be a key conduit for dissent on a range of political, economic, ecological and cultural issues during the early 2000s (Atton, 2004). During the 2000 Sydney Olympics, for instance, Indymedia was a focus for critique regarding the staging of the Olympics as well as a source for alternative news and perspectives regarding national affairs in Australia.

Indymedia can easily be perceived as a species of alternative media. Clearly it is undertaken by a group of loosely linked people who have some common interest and agenda. In contrast to restricted experiments in collaborative news by non-professional journalists, there have also been many ventures involving professional journalists. One of the earliest such open-news initiatives, and the one most often referred to, is South Korea's OhmyNews. Started in 1999 by the relatively unknown journalist Oh Yeon-Ho under the rubric, 'Every Citizen Is a Reporter', OhmyNews was launched in early 2000 (Joyce, 2007). Within a few years of its establishment, it was the top Korean online news site, highly ranked among all news outlets and judged as decisive in the 2002 election of President Roh Moo-Hyun (Joyce, 2007; Nguyen, 2010; Young, 2009). OhmyNews commenced an English-language version (2004–6), which was relaunched as OhmyNews International (OMNI), complete with a Twitter version, focusing on the discussion of citizen journalism and the aggregation of content from around the world.

'Grassroots journalism, citizen media, crowdsourcing are all related terms that tackle the same question: How are regular people making and changing the news?' (OMNI, 2010). The rationale for the rebadged OMNI approach was born of the need to deal with its international success as a leader in citizen journalism:

> With citizen reporters from every corner of the world writing on every topic imaginable, it became increasingly difficult to cover stories consistently ... . With stories coming from places like Afghanistan, Brazil, Zimbabwe and everywhere in-between, it was impossible for our editors to accurately check each story. Fact-checking is one of our core principles.
>
> (OMNI, 2010)

Nguyen argues that 'OhmyNews is essentially a hybrid news cooperative based on a cleverly, creatively managed marriage between citizen reporters and trained, skilled and experienced journalists, which is fundamental to its success' (Nguyen, 2010, p. 196). Nguyen notes that:

OhmyNews is not of the same type as 'publish then filter' participatory news sites such as NowPublic and Wikinews, where users' content is freely posted before being fact-checked, corrected and edited by other users. All OhmyNews citizen stories go though a thorough screening process by full-time journalists in its central Seoul newsroom, who retain the ultimate authority and right to reject or edit contributions.

(Nguyen, 2010, p. 202)

The OhmyNews model is still built upon citizen-contributed content (an estimated 70 per cent of stories), as well as on a relatively transparent and open newsroom:

As soon as a person's identity is substantiated, he or she is allocated a reporter desk, from which he or she can go anywhere in the virtual newsroom .... If he or she has concerns over some editorial decisions, there is a public forum in which to share his or her views with fellow reporters and staff editors. Moreover, editors have the duty to publicly justify why they reject stories. Additionally, there is an ombudsman committee, made up of citizen reporters and external observers, to monitor OhmyNews stories every day.

(Nguyen, 2010, p. 204)

The need for a nuanced approached to understanding OhmyNews, rather than assuming it to be a relatively straightforward instance of alternative media, based on available Western models, had been earlier asserted in a study that dubbed its practice 'hybrid progressive-commercial':

On the one hand, OhmyNews includes a wide range of news on society, politics, the economy and culture, replicating the omnibus format of Western consumerist newspapers. Yet, on the other hand, OhmyNews relies extensively on its network of 'citizen reporters' for contributions, significantly extending a dimension of participation in the news production process beyond the norm of commercial publications.

(Kim and Hamilton, 2006, p. 542)

In their evaluation of OhmyNews, Kim and Hamilton remind us that 'signs such as a broader demographic range of contributors should not be taken as automatic proof that democratic communication has been achieved' (Kim and Hamilton, 2006, p. 557).

As well as the alternative and independent movements around news, the new entrants challenging the power of the established news agencies are the web and search-based news aggregators. The internet had brought vast amounts of information and news into the purview of users. With the advent of the web, the amount of material exponentially increased, but so too did the technologies for finding and distributing it. Search technologies such as Google, Yahoo! and Baidu have grown in importance because they have provided algorithmic methods for identifying and locating information. Apparently radical customization of news became possible, with the interlocking of different internet technologies. Theoretically it is possible for each person to have their 'daily me' – their own unique, customized news feed. The 'daily me' was an idea developed at the MIT Lab through its experiments in personalized news from the early 1980s onwards (Bender, 2002). Actually a version of the 'daily me' is relatively simple to achieve through combinations of RSS feeds, tailored websites (iGoogle), online alerts (for instance, Google Alerts), mobile alerts (via text messaging), Twitter and so on (Dwyer, 2010). An early issue raised about such personalization is the possibility of missing out on news that does not fit one's profile (assigned or chosen) (Harper, 1999). News aggregation can occur through human, editorial selection in sites such as *Drudge Report*, *Huffington Post* and others – which also carry or commission their own content. The large search and internet companies developed their own news aggregators, which operate algorithmically on principles of automation, such as Google News, MSN, Yahoo! and AOL:

> Even though these sites produced no actual journalism themselves, they functioned as 'aggregators', collecting links and leads from other news sources, filtering them into topical categories (e.g., headlines, sports, entertainment, politics, etc.), and presenting them on the main pages of the most high-traffic sites on the web.
>
> (Scott, 2005, pp. 94–5)

A number of scholars point to the very real limits in the ability of most people to make, organize and consume news the way they wish to:

> Internet audiences are primarily an extension of the main legacy media brand outlets ... breaking news aggregators link to legacy media sources who originate the material. In this sense they are vulture-like in that they have not invested in the costly 'hunting and gathering'

required for news production, especially time-intensive investigative material.

                                                          (Dwyer, 2010, pp. 51–2)

The harbinger of what was to come was that the agencies, which had long reigned over international news were able to dominate the new distribution network early on:

> Associated Press and Reuters became major players, supplying ideally suited digital content (i.e., short and sweet) to the portal aggregators, start-up news websites, and traditional news vendors looking to strengthen their online presence. Through sophisticated content management systems (CMSs), which could be mapped onto their existing systems, a company like Reuters could take better advantage of their 2,300 reporters in 160 countries ... this sea of data no longer need pass across an editor's desk but is entered by reporters into a commonly accessible, networked database.
>
>   (Scott, 2005, p. 95)

As these sceptical perspectives on the actual diversity of news sources reveal, the efforts to create new paradigms, organizations, processes and institutions in news have had varying degrees of success. Taken together, what they aim to displace is the hegemony of established news agencies over what is regarded and published as news. However, news as it exists in the press and across mainstream media is a highly structured undertaking – something that often passes the news consumer's notice. The debate over the source of news and the influence of news agencies can usefully be considered in the context of changes in the roles and practices associated with newsrooms.

Clearly, the nature of news gathering, journalism and media work has altered with the advent of new technologies. Journalists are now expected to routinely recast, if not conceive, their work for multimedia, cross-platform delivery, while media corporations and organizations invest heavily in systems, training and policies to support this new idea of the press. Where this emphasis on technology and the media is most evident is at the very epicentre of journalism and news – the newsroom. The idea of the newsroom has long functioned as the celebrated place where journalism, its organization and socialization are forged. The subordinate place that women still have in journalism can be explained by recourse to the culture, habits and structure of the newsroom (North, 2009; Poindexter, Meraz and Weiss, 2008). As many discussions of journalism reveal, the newsroom often stands in for journalism itself. Journalism and journalists, it is believed, are forged in the newsroom. Any meaningful change needs to be gauged there also – though its centrality has been contested, and no more so than through the contemporary trends in news and journalism (Wahl-Jorgensen, 2010). As part of this process of the remaking and displacing of the newsroom, we find that the 'digital' or 'convergent' newsroom is being put in place in leading newspapers and broadcasters with quite some fanfare.

The intensification of technology in the newsroom has been something that has been underway for quite some decades. Leading scholar of online, convergent newsrooms Pablo Boczkowski has noted that the 'computerization of newsrooms has been one of the most pervasive transformations in American media organizations since the 1970s' (Boczkowski, 2004b, p. 198), – and it is likely that this is the case in many other countries also. Amid these changes to newsrooms in which digital technologies are crucial are some interesting continuities. Much national and international news is provided by news agencies. News agencies such as Associated Press, Reuters and others take news from freelance journalists, agency staff and a range of other media workers, and combine this into a news feed to which media organizations subscribe. Much of the news published by the press comprises short – and sometimes longer – items taken from the 'wires' (or feeds from news agencies). This is especially the case for organizations or areas of news where there is an insufficient number of dedicated journalists or organizational imperatives, to independently report, research and cover news. Interestingly, a great deal of online news provided by major organizations is reworked material from news agencies. A study of the Al-Jazeera English newsroom in Kuala Lumpur – the English-language arm of the acclaimed Qatar-based broadcaster which, in the wake of the events of September 11, 2001, and the threat posed by the terrorist group Al-Qaeda, drew large audiences and achieved some infamy across both the Arabic-speaking and non-Arab world – has shown that online journalists' work revolved around redacting news-agency items, compared to the emphasis placed by television editors and journalist colleagues on independent reporting and news values (Domingo and Paterson, 2011; Wei, 2010). Thus the debate over the organization of news, its sources, and how they are drawn upon, continues. With new technologies come new possibilities for diversifying and extending news through experiments like OhmyNews, set alongside the enduring power and flexible responses of long-established news agencies (Domingo and Paterson, 2011). Intriguingly what emerge are the alliances forged across new and old media, a tribute to the ductible nature of media itself. It is these accommodations and transactions between the old and new that characterize the media's adaptation to new technologies.

Wikinews and the Battle of the Filters

As we have seen so far, online news has as extensive history, stretching back to at least the early 1980s. Online news intensifies with the appearance of the web and the great rise of the commercial, mass internet in the 1990s. Existing private and public media organizations engage heavily with models of online news. Alternative models of news are devised, such as open news, citizen journalism and other models we have noted. Upon closer inspection, many of these alternative models often turn out to be reliant upon, or at least interacting with, established journalism and news. In this light, one of the most furiously debated recent models, WikiLeaks, warrants an extended discussion – not only because of its stunning irruption into the mainstream of international news, but because it represents an exemplary, if intricate, story of how new technologies and the media can play out.

The Wiki is an internet technology that allows collaborative authoring and editing of documents and material, and display of these on a Wiki site. The greatest achievement in the world of Wikis is Wikipedia. Wikipedia is the heavily consulted yet much decried online encyclopedia, which relies upon distributed, volunteer composition, checking and correction of entries. Another well-publicized initiative of the Wiki Media Foundation in 2004 was the launch of the Wikinews project (Glasner, 2004). Still active in 2011, Wikinews uses the collaborative Wiki model and describes itself as a 'free content news source [project] … that seeks to provide content, free of charge, where everyone is invited to contribute reports about events large and small, either from direct experience, or summarized from elsewhere' (Wikinews, 2010). Wikinews is based upon the same principles as Wikipedia: 'neutral, free content, and open decision-making processes' (Wikinews, 2010). Wikinews, however, has been eclipsed by another Wiki-named project – WikiLeaks.

WikiLeaks is an independent, non-profit organization, launched in 2006, that publishes news documents from anonymous news sources and leaks. WikiLeaks made a big impression very quickly, receiving an Index on Censorship Freedom of Expression award in 2008 (Index on

Censorship, 2008). WikiLeaks made available directly to the public the kind of documents traditionally leaked by the press, and, as time went on, it certainly did more than its fair share of this. What is novel is that it also made public the new kinds of data government and corporate agencies were able to record and store – that previously would neither have been regarded as worthy of release for the scrutiny of citizens, nor as sources for journalists. In late 2009, for instance, WikiLeaks released a set of data containing a distinctive record of the events of the terrorist attacks of 9/11:

> WikiLeaks released half a million US national text pager intercepts. The intercepts cover a 24-hour period surrounding the September 11, 2001 attacks in New York and Washington ... . The archive is a completely objective record of the defining moment of our time. We hope that its entrance into the historical record will lead to a nuanced understanding of how this event led to death, opportunism and war.
>
> (http://mirror.wikileaks.info/wiki/911/)

At this time, WikiLeaks declared its intentions:

> Our primary interest is in exposing oppressive regimes in Asia, the former Soviet bloc, sub-Saharan Africa and the Middle East, but we are of assistance to people of all nations who wish to reveal unethical behavior in their governments and corporations ... . WikiLeaks opens leaked documents up to stronger scrutiny than any media organization or intelligence agency can provide. WikiLeaks provides a forum for the entire global community to relentlessly examine any document for its credibility, plausibility, veracity and validity.
>
> (Visser, 2009)

In the next year, WikiLeaks released an enormous amount of material, with three particular releases attracting much controversy.

In April 2010, WikiLeaks released a classified 2007 US military video showing an Apache helicopter attacking and killing a group of Iraqi civilians. While the initial public reaction was generally one of unalloyed horror at the brutality of the US attack, the backlash was not only confined to the US government. A range of commentators – including comedian Stephen Colbert in a much-noted interview with Assange – questioned the emotional manipulation and de-contextualization of the video as it was edited for release (Kennedy, 2010). WikiLeaks modified its tactics with its July 2010 release of the US military internal logs of the Afghanistan conflict dated 2004–9. It struck an agreement with the *Guardian*, *New York Times* and *Der Spiegel* to simultaneously publish their reports regarding the Afghanistan war logs, at the same time as WikiLeaks released the full database on the internet (*Guardian*, 2010). One reason WikiLeaks turned to these lions of the established press was to bolster its reputation for accurate and responsible journalism, something that was only partially successful (Kennedy, 2010). The release of this secret material elicited the expected condemnation from the US government, its military, security agencies and allies. However, WikiLeaks also attracted strong criticism from journalists and organizations defending press freedom for carelessly releasing the names of many Afghani informants assisting coalition forces. Reporters without Borders and Amnesty International were two respected organizations that criticized WikiLeaks for failing to redact names of individuals at risk from the release of the documents (Siddique, 2010). WikiLeaks rejected the criticisms at the time, but later took these on board (for a time at least) – as was evident in its most sensational and long-running release yet: the voluminous US embassy cables.

Released from November 2010 onwards, with fresh revelations pertinent to various countries unfolding daily, these were 251,287 diplomatic cables from 250 US embassies around the world containing the candid assessments of officials of foreign governments. The material caused severe discomfit to many governments around the world too numerous to mention. With the US embassy cables, WikiLeaks again struck agreements with leading press outlets. There were many advantages to this, including the ability to take advantage of the fact-checking, analysis and interpretation skills of leading journalists. Also the newspapers were able to pick out the aspects of the cables most germane to their national publics, and zero in on the points of maximum embarrassment and outrage to their own governments. Last but not least, when Assange was being threatened with assassination and imprisonment by figures in the US establishment, and WikiLeaks itself was being hounded, he was able to point to the fact that others – highly regarded newspapers no less – had also published the cables. In fascinating ways, we see Assange's WikiLeaks cloaking itself in the honourable traditions of the Fourth Estate, refining its claims to practices of truth-telling. Elsewhere Assange, with a flourish, termed this approach 'scientific journalism':

In 1958 a young Rupert Murdoch, then owner and editor of Adelaide's *The News*, wrote: 'In the race between secrecy and truth, it seems inevitable that truth will always win' ... . I grew up in a Queensland country town where people spoke their minds bluntly. They distrusted big government as something that could be corrupted if not watched carefully ... . WikiLeaks was created around these core values. The idea, conceived in Australia, was to use internet technologies in new ways to report the truth. WikiLeaks coined a new type of journalism: scientific journalism. We work with other media outlets to bring people the news, but also to prove it is true. Scientific journalism allows you to read a news story, then to click online to see the original document it is based on. That way you can judge for yourself: Is the story true? Did the journalist report it accurately? Democratic societies need a strong media and WikiLeaks is part of that media.

(Kennedy, 2010)

In late 2010, the British High Court upheld a decision to allow Julian Assange bail pending extradition proceedings for a potential rape charge in Sweden. While Assange was engulfed by legal battles, Icelandic investigative journalist Kristin Hrafnsson became the spokesperson for WikiLeaks (Greenberg, 2010). While working for the national broadcaster, RUV, Hrafnsson had reported on the collapse of Iceland's Kaupthing Bank, which caused his TV programme to be taken off air and his team to be sacked. Subsequently he was involved in a struggle against legal suppression of further exposés about the bank, based on documents made available through WikiLeaks. Hrafnsson also served as an external advisor to Icelandic Modern Media Initiative, in its fascinating efforts to give Iceland the most expansive free speech and whistleblower laws. When he subsequently left the national broadcaster, Hrafnsson collaborated with WikiLeaks, eventually joining the organization and becoming its spokesperson. An important aspect of his mandate was to shift WikiLeaks away from being synonymous with the identity and at times unpredictable views of Assange. Further, as a respected journalist, Hrafnsson had much more credibility than Assange in putting the case for WikiLeaks to be regarded as a journalism and news organization.

Through 2011, the fate of WikiLeaks itself hung in the balance, as it continued to release documents with its press partners. In the meantime, various governments decried the organization, and tried to find ways to close it down. As I have suggested, during this time, WikiLeaks has moved from being a radical outlier, experimenting with the potential of the internet to create a new media force, to becoming something that works hand-in-glove with the respectable organs of the press that it hoped to trump through its 'higher scrutiny'. It is not only governments that have assailed the transparency of WikiLeaks. The *modus operandi* of WikiLeaks has been questioned by a range of independent commentators and civil-society figures, who otherwise support its aims, as well as by former collaborators (Domscheit-Berg, 2011). Despite the efforts of WikiLeaks' various collaborators and supporters, troubling gaps remain in its rationale as an important new form of media organization. In comparison to OhmyNews, for instance, it has lacked the openness and detailed working through of how to apply journalistic norms to the material it is given and then releases. This is a great irony, of course, given that WikiLeaks' overriding value is openness of information in the face of the world. While Assange has proven a master of the dark arts of postmodern media celebrity, especially with his many mainstream media appearances, his lapidary utterances have not sufficed to quell the doubts. The organization continues to zig and zag its way through the moral and ethical minefields of pioneering raw data journalism.

A low point in the annals of WikiLeaks came with its September 2010 release of its entire cache of over 251,000 US diplomatic cables in unredacted form. The documents identified activists, whistleblowers and informants. The password giving access to the cache was accidentally published by *Guardian* reporters in their book on WikiLeaks (Leigh and Harding, 2011). After a complicated chain of events involving various WikiLeaks activists, current and former, the password and cache of files became available elsewhere. WikiLeaks then decided to make the cache available itself, blaming the *Guardian* for the breach of security. Others, however, blamed Assange for sloppy procedures, evident in his careless re-use of a master password in collaborations with the *Guardian* journalists during 2010. In any case, WikiLeaks' release of the unedited cache was condemned by the five newspapers – *Guardian*, *New York Times*, *El País*, *Der Spiegel* and *Le Monde* – that had worked with WikiLeaks during the previous year selecting and editing various documents before release (Ball, 2011).

Ironically, the debate over the ethics of this finale to WikiLeaks 'cablegate' was overshadowed by the continuing furore over the *News Limited* phone-hacking scandal. Alongside its coverage of WikiLeaks' release of the full cache of cables, for instance, the *Guardian* website carried an ad for its 29 September 2011 debate entitled 'After Hacking: How Can the Press Restore Trust?', featuring such luminaries as Carl Bernstein, who was co-winner of the Pulitzer Prize for his coverage of

President Nixon's Watergate scandal (*Guardian*, 2011). Clearly, old and new media struggle in their own ways with the moral dimensions of making the news.

High Stakes of Mobile News

As we have seen, throughout its history the business models underpinning online news have waxed and waned. Early on in the development of online news, established press interests hoped that readers would be happy to pay. However, very few subscriptions models for newspapers have been successful. The outstanding exception is the financial press – where the now international *Financial Times* continues to command a premium for its print edition, and also to attract subscribers for its online edition (bundled with the print version also). A number of leading newspapers around the world – such as the *New York Times* – stabilized their online offerings around free access to latest and recent content (up to, say, seven days). After that, if a reader wishes to access articles from the archive, then they need to pay (or do so through a library database, if they have access). Because of the dynamics of the internet and search, however, it is often possible to Google an article – and retrieve it from a cache or another website. Some well-known newspapers have eschewed the pay-for-content model entirely, and allow free access to current content and to the archive, such as the *Guardian*. Underpinning such decisions is a punt on a different business model – for instance, the idea that online consumption of newspaper material will generate advertising revenue, or contribute to other product or revenue streams; or that online parts of the newspaper will boost brand visibility and recognition. In 2009, the battle for the commercial future of online news took a new turn, however, with the boom in the e-reader, smartphone and tablet computer markets.

The skirmishes over online news quickly intensified into a war over mobile news. Mobile news started with SMS alerts and news, though its potential had been discussed and prototypes developed before this (Pavlik, 2001). With the rise of premium-rate mobile services, as well as mobile data and content services in general, a wide range of mobile news services became available. Major newspaper companies especially took an interest in the possibilities of mobile news, as part of their overall online news strategies – as did the *Irish Times* (Cawley, 2008). Many newspapers make it easy to receive alerts and news via SMS. Most major newspapers now offer news via mobiles, and there are significant initiatives underway with mobile news in a range of countries (notably South Korea, where mobile television has been most popular). The motto of the *New York Times* echoes the common refrain in contemporary media of user control of time and mode of consumption: 'Enjoy the high-quality journalism of the *New York Times* whenever and on whatever device you desire' (*New York Times*, 2009).

The advent of the iPhone in 2007 meant that there was now a popular mobile phone that functioned quite well as an e-reader or e-book device. The *New York Times*'s 'All the news that's fit to print' becomes 'All the news that's fit to go', in their iPhone application – 'A new way to take your news with you'. Here the iPhone promises to extend the mobile news browsing and selection experience, making it more customizable and with a higher resolution – rather than ushering in a radically different experience. One subscriber benefit offered by many newspapers – for instance, the *Financial Times*, as well as the *Guardian* and others – is the facsimile of the paper made available online, including on a mobile. The urge to '[s]ee the paper exactly as it was printed' would appear to be a confected artefact of continuity in the midst of the new media ecology being created here (Boczkowski, 2004a). The third version of the Amazon Kindle e-reader, announced in May 2009, featured a much wider screen, especially customized for newspaper reading. Another major entrant into the portable, mobile-media market was Google's Android operating system. It quickly established itself across many handsets and devices as a fertile platform for apps.

Some press proprietors were very clear at the outset about portable and mobile media representing a long-overdue opportunity to make readers pay for online news. Take, for instance, Rupert Murdoch's opening sally:

> 'I can assure you, we will not be sending our content rights to the fine people who created the Kindle,' he said. 'We will control the prices for our content, and we will control the relationship with our customers.'
>
> (*Guardian*, 2009)

Not for the first time in the history of the internet, Murdoch claimed that the 'current days of the internet will soon be over' (*Guardian*, 2009) – this time with good reason. Mobile devices offer new features, media forms and content that reinvent newspapers for multimedia. From a commercial perspective what is especially felicitous about mobiles is that they provide robust systems for billing, licensing and controlling content.

Murdoch's hopes were soon realized with the appearance in early 2010 of Apple's iPad – the media-consumption device, conceived to compete with e-readers, tablets, laptops and a range of other personal and portable media. The iPad is but one of a number of e-reader tablet devices that promise an easier transition from the cultural technology of the newspaper, well accepted by its users, to an electronic form. Availing themselves of the success of Apple's apps culture (Goggin, 2011c), many newspapers quickly offered monthly subscriptions via an app – for a price competitive with the price offering (or bundled in with the print subscriptions). Others sought to create new kinds of newspapers using apps. In late 2010, Murdoch publicized his plan to launch a national newspaper in the US, distributed as paid content via the iPad and mobile phone (Pilkington, 2010). The newspaper would target young readers, pooling content from outlets across the News Corp. stable. Operating under the *New York Post*, it would offer shorter, snappier stories and compete directly with established titles such as the *New York Times*: ' "We'll have young people reading newspapers," the 79-year-old Murdoch said during the company's Aug. 4 earnings call. "It's a real game changer in the presentation of news" ' (*LA Times*, 2010).

As yet, there have been few examples of interesting or successful new newspapers using mobile-media platforms – somewhat curious, given the range of innovative experiments with online news. Instead, well-established newspaper titles have extended and adapted their editions for delivery and reading on smartphones and tablets.

While still evolving, newspaper editions designed for the reading experience of iPads and other tablets are markedly different from print, online and previous mobile subscriptions. To a reader accustomed to the content and facilities of either the print or online edition, early newspaper apps for tablets tended to contain less content and to organize it differently. Some newspapers simply offered a lightly customized digital facsimile of the main daily editions – often with some sections of the paper missing. By 2012, distinctive features of newspaper editions for tablets had emerged, just as they had previously with online news. Various newspapers now make a considerable effort to ensure that their main sections are available. Subscribers to the *New York Times*, for instance, can also choose from print, tablet, smartphone and e-reader for computer versions – or pay to have combinations of all of these. When reading a newspaper on the iPad, one is struck by the colour, resolution and impact of the images – indeed photojournalism is undergoing a renaissance with newspaper apps. Multimedia also feature prominently, as readers can click on video stories as well as reading text or looking at images. More than anything, advertising for the iPad and other tablets shows great potential. The nature of navigation on apps means that advertising is more prominent and 'sticky' than in newspapers or online. When clicking through the articles, a featured advertisement appears that needs to be dismissed with a click before the desired content can be viewed. Moreover, advertisements can incorporate very high-quality graphics and video, and consumers can click through to full-colour brochures of products and services. (Not surprisingly the resilient media form of magazines has blossomed on iPads and tablets, with something of a dichotomy emerging between apps of large-circulation magazines, on the one hand, and carefully produced, artisanal print editions of small-circulation magazines, on the other (LeMasurier, 2012).) In the case of newspapers, while some attempt has been made to incorporate features of social media into newspaper apps (sharing links with friends, for instance, and bookmarking), there are far fewer of the supplementary and interactive features of online websites that users now expect – whether this be easy searching or access to archives, message boards and posting comments.

Newspaper apps, and mobile news in general, represent a still-evolving media form. More than simply offering new reader experiences and ways to present the news, mobile devices and networks stand to be vitally important for the development of online news and their underlying business models. Newspaper apps are being eagerly watched to see if they will provide a viable revenue stream to prop up newspapers, as they suffer the near-mortal blow of loss of advertising. Apps are part of a reinvigorated attempt to settle upon a business model that will finally see consumers pay for digital content. The two most prominent recent attempts to construct 'paywalls' around newspaper content have been those of the *New York Times* (whose app we have just encountered) and London's equally prestigious *Times* newspaper. In 2009, new media maven Arianna Huffington declared the 'paywall is history', declaring that

> journalism's best days lie ahead – so long as we embrace innovation and don't try to pretend that we can somehow hop into a journalistic Way Back Machine and return to a past that no longer exists and can't be resurrected.
>
> (Huffington, 2009)

Two years on, the paywall debate raged on – with some signs, however, that consumers were now prepared to pay for online news. In its first quarter of the new prices, the 'old gray lady' (as the *New York Times* is fondly known), claimed that it had 224,000 digital subscribers to nytimes.com, 57,000 iPad and Kindle users and 750,000 print subscribers registering for online access (Preston, 2011). In addition, the newspaper reported that online advertising had increased by 16 per cent. In comparison, *The Times* reported 100,000 subscribers to its £2 a week digital subscription in the first year of operation (Sabbagh, 2011) – something that commentators judged a 'faint success' (Gillmor, 2011). Thus, while the advent of apps, and the mobile media that now represent the future of online, are yielding some revenue, indications are that this still will not suffice. Revenue from print editions looks set to provide the bulk of newspaper funds for some years to come. And the problem with this is that neither print or digital sales, nor online advertising, are increasing fast enough to cover the serious decline in advertising revenue. Thus the way that mobile and online news unfolds, and how this plays out with the imperatives now facing newspapers, press and media companies, will be an instructive contrast – telling us much about the politics and possibilities of new technologies and the media.

While the major titles sought to reconfigure both the traditional and online forms of their newspapers for the new mobile media, mobile apps were being used for another form of news: social media. As we have seen, an important development in the media has been the role of the user in activating internet and mobile technology to gather, filter and disseminate news – from newsgroups and email, through websites and blogs, to mobile news. The emergence of social-networking systems and the range of applications clustered under the broad label of social media have only deepened the interactions between established, mainstream media and alternative, online sources – as has occurred with blogs. There are now many important social-media applications playing a significant part in the creation and consumption of news, not least Facebook. However, recently it has been the micro-blogging applications around the world that have followed hot on the heels of blogs in making their mark on established news – especially Twitter.

Launched in 2006, the short-messaging, interactive broadcasting system Twitter claimed over 200 million users by 2011. Like SMS, Twitter only allows 'Tweets' (messages) of 140 characters, which can then be read by followers. Like blogs and other internet media, Twitter initially gained prominence as a platform for anyone to contribute their thoughts, and gain an audience. Its use by celebrities, in particular, became a novel feature, which allowed ordinary people the sense of being directly in contact with a favourite star by following them, and having the thrill of being followed in turn. A backlash against the banality and inconsequentiality of many Tweets, not to mention the flood of quotidian information, saw Twitter refine its own guidance to users: 'Some people find it useful to contribute their own Tweets, but the real magic of Twitter lies in absorbing real-time information that matters to you' (Twitter, 2011). I won't discuss here the way that Twitter has contributed to the broadening of what is regarded as news – for instance, the importance of small circles, the private sphere, the everyday and the intimate as key contexts for news. What I want to note briefly is the growing importance of Twitter in the established economy of news.

In the period I have been discussing when the mobile internet burgeoned, courtesy of smartphones and other devices, Twitter became widely used by journalists, news organizations and citizen producers of news. The advantage of Twitter is its ability to work across platforms, allowing users to Tweet, check their feed, and reTweet from apps, browsers and SMS on mobile devices, as well as computers. Many news organizations now Tweet their news updates regularly, leading to new 'source cycles' among Twitters users, as well as other online, mobile, electronic media and print media forms. The other outstanding way in which Twitter has wrought changes is via the capacity it affords users to aggregate their own news. Via the simple hash tag, users can tag their Tweet – to categorize it thematically. Other users can then search by the hash tag – for #WikiLeaks, for instance – to find all the Tweets on this subject that interest them (Lindgren and Lundström, 2011). These patterns of dissemination can provide new channels for news, a development with potentially profound implications.

The importance of Twitter and other social media for contemporary news was dramatized by the brutal deaths of two people in Mexico in September 2011, killed by the drug cartels for their social-media reportage. It had come to international notice in 2010 that bloggers and Tweeters in Mexico were providing news and information on the drug wars in that country, because traditional journalists and media, having suffered many deaths and ongoing violence, were limiting their coverage (Tuchman, 2010). In late August 2011, two Twitter users faced thirty years in prison, after the state of Veracruz arrested them on terrorism and sabotage charges for spreading rumours concerning an attack by drug gangs on a primary school (Hernandez, 2011). While this bizarre case played out, the *narcotraficantes* (drug traffickers) had no doubt about the newsworthiness of coverage of various blogs, Twitter accounts and hash tags. The testament to this was the shocking spectacle of the bodies of the two people awfully treated – a woman and a man – left hanging from a bridge in the border city of Nuevo Laredo, bearing placards threatening those who report incidents via social media (specifically naming the *Al Rojo Vivo* and *Blog del Vivo* blogs) (Castillo, 2011). These terrible deaths remind us that amid the transformations and debates surrounding new technologies, we cannot take the media, old or new, for granted. In so many ways, the stakes can be very high indeed.

4 Broadcasting Media and the Social Turn

> The future of television is to stop thinking of television as television.
> Nicholas Negroponte (Negroponte, 1995)

> TV is breaking out of the box on to your smartphone or tablet, wherever you are and whenever you want it.
> Fiona Graham (Graham, 2011)

> We are reinventing television.
> Sony Corporation advertisement, *c.* 2012

The idea of broadcasting is still evoked for many by the television set ensconced in the lounge, or the radio set recessed in the kitchen window or gracing the bedroom dresser. Yet the histories of broadcasting offer us many different images of what this central form of media does, means and offers. Broadcasting achieved something like a stable identity in the second half of the twentieth century – allowing John F. Kennedy, who led the US in the early 1960s, to be dubbed the 'first television president' (Berry, 1987).

Even as late as the last years of the twentieth century, broadcasting served, for some at least, to define the spirit of the age, with scholarly talk of the 'television age' that would have an odd ring now. In the last few years, broadcasting has experienced profound, rapid and clamorous transformation. At the heart of the dynamics of change and persistence that characterize broadcasting, we once again find technology (Mullan, 1997). If new technologies are heavily implicated in the contemporary press, this is even more the case when it comes to broadcasting. With digital technologies, and media convergence, television programmes can be watched or listened to via many platforms, on a range of devices, at the time and place of a viewer's choosing. Television is going through a fascinating, fertile renaissance in a 'post-broadcast' world, in which the once powerful networks, regulators and government interests that controlled the 'tube' have been thoroughly chastened.

In this light, then, this chapter introduces the forms and issues of the new technology reshaping broadcasting. First, it is important to understand what the media use of households now looks like, and where television fits in. So I begin with a map of the media ecologies of the household. The video recorder introduced viewers to the idea of recording and playing back television. This was followed by the technology of the digital video player (DVD), and then the digital video recorder (DVR). Once these devices were added to the new possibilities allowed by digital formats, digital TV sets and the internet, consumer choice was greatly extended. The new horizons of television are represented by technologies such as TiVo (allowing viewers to find and choose their television programmes, rather than having them dictated by the broadcaster), and the presence of media centres in households (networked computer servers that gather and distribute content to domestic users). The same applies to listening technologies, where computers, servers and advanced stereos aggregate the many possibilities. Regardless of whether 'convergence' is occurring, the reality now is that listeners have a range of technologies to choose from: analogue radio, digital audio broadcasting or internet radio. For a long time, reception had been portable with radio receivers, and now digital reception is also mobile, with consumers downloading audio or radio programmes onto an iPod ('podcasting') or digital music player. Or listeners use a mobile phone for retrieving broadcast content (perhaps purchased through iTunes, rather than downloaded). Failing that, they can listen to or watch a broadcast on a mobile-media or wireless device (phone, hand-held, laptop, tablet).

From household use of digital media and its implications for broadcasting, I move, in the second section of the chapter, to the development of digital television. A classic task in understanding new media technology is deciphering the struggles they attract when introduced – especially, as we saw in Chapter 2, when it comes to the standards that are adopted. Here the long awaited technology of digital television took shape in a long, hard-fought battle among groups of industry, government, regulators and equipment manufacturers. A fascinating development from these industrial and economic battles over television, like other new digital technologies, is that the radio waves themselves – what we call 'spectrum' – have emerged as a shared concern and resource. Finally, I look at the most interesting and unpredictable element in the puzzle of new technology and television: the user. It is only more recently that viewers and the communities of which they form part have been able to have much of a say in influencing the shape and social relations of television. Now, however, the user (what he or she may be) cannot be ignored. Without warning, or perhaps even precedent, users have availed themselves of internet-based technologies and cultures to reconfigure television. Hence the love affair that technology companies are pleading for with their users. I argue that in this 'user' turn in television, we can find subtle and far-reaching logics unfolding. In one prominent take on contemporary television, the traditional idea of the broadcast relationship – from broadcaster to viewer – is seen as being displaced by ideas such as 'social television'. Here television is recomposed from a medley of protocols – digital video broadcast, standard terrestrial broadcast, mobile, web 2.0, IP TV, Bluetooth, iPhone apps. More than this, television itself, it is argued, is created from the networks of the groups of viewers and taste communities that recommend, rate, swap and create televisual experiences. This is television being built from lateral associations, it is suggested, rather than the formerly hierarchical relationships between the broadcasters (the one central source) and the public (the many), only knowable through ratings.

Before commencing, however, it is important to remind the reader of the overarching issue about new media and technology outlined in Chapter 2. Like the other major media forms discussed in this book, it is necessary to speak of television to some extent as a single global phenomenon. However, it is important also to recognize that television, like newspapers, or the internet, has looked very different, to particular groups of people, in different places and at different times. This was the case with analogue television, however obscured by assumptions that television represented undiluted cultural imperialism in countries in which it arrived. It is happening all over again with digital television (Bennett and Strange, 2011). Despite declarations of regional deadlines for the shutdown of analogue TV, many countries have already done this, or are well underway with it – while many other countries do not have digital at all. This point about the specific forms that television takes in different places is well made by Graeme Turner and Jinna Tay in their analysis of the international take-up of cable, free-to-air, satellite and digital television where they urge us to acknowledge 'the sheer diversity of the ways in which the futures of broadcast, pay, and online video play out in different nation-states and geo-linguistic regional markets' (Turner and Tay, 2010, p. 37).

Watching Television with Households of the Future

A classic place to come to grips with the manner in which new technologies are influencing television media is in the scrutiny of the household. Television is watched by billions of people globally and forms an intimate part of the small worlds of householders and the relationships that they have with each other, others in their society and distant others elsewhere. Television broadcasters, programme makers, advertisers and equipment manufacturers invest substantial funds and much effort into understanding what people watch (Gitlin, 1994). The television industry and groups of researchers have for some decades put a great deal of effort into systems of rating programmes. Television ratings, therefore, have been the principal way that advertisers are reassured that their promotions for products and services are reaching audiences. For scholars also, the household has been a favoured locale, with many different approaches employed. Critical questions for this research include: how television is viewed, the contexts in which this occurs, the meanings attributed to it, how consumption happens and what relationship is forged between a household's use of the television and other spheres of everyday life, media and culture (Alasuutari, 1999). Television has been a decisive form in the emergence of audience theory in cultural and media studies (Ang, 1991; Morley, 1992), with many famous studies including Ien Ang's work on the 1980s globally received soap opera *Dallas* (1978–91) (Ang, 1991) and Charlotte Brunsdon and David Morley's classic research on the British television programme *Nationwide* (1969–83) (Brunsdon and Morley, 1978; Morley, 1980). What this research reveals is that households have a powerful influence on television and its meanings, rather than, as is often assumed, television causing its viewers to do and think particular things. Households have their own dynamics and are involved in significant social, economic and political transformations. It is important to realize this before turning to the new media form of television. For its part, technology forms a central part of today's households, embroidered into the patterns that create, reproduce and sustain them. When it comes to television, we find that technology is now becoming a force, for both change and conservation of past ways, in especially significant ways. Not least, the ways in which households and individuals use and consume television – an intricate yet powerful phenomenon – are something that the producers of television can no longer ignore.

For its first few decades, television broadcasting has consisted of signals beamed into a receiver (or set), which needed to be watched as they were broadcast. The signal could neither be stored in the set, nor captured by another device and replayed at a later time (at least without recourse to relatively difficult-to-use recording equipment). The breakthrough in recording technology came once video recorders became available to the consumer market. The first videotape recorder was publicly demonstrated in 1951 (Howett, 2006). Video recording has been used in television production and broadcast since the late 1950s. Originally, television shows were broadcast live and preserved in monochrome (black and white) using film kinescope. From 1957 onwards, black-and-white videotape was used to record live programmes, then from 1958 colour videotape started to take over (for an example involving the Edsel show, see Trexler, 2007). Before the advent of satellite television and high bandwidth networks, videos were shipped by air in order that programmes could be shared across a country. Truly portable colour television cameras and recorders using video were not widely used until the mid-1970s (Howett, 2006). Despite this, from a relatively early time, videotape technology used in production and broadcast found its way into the domestic market:

> Tape revolutionized TV broadcasting. Now it's going to revolutionize TV watching. The first video tape recorder for home use will hit the American market next year. Developed in England, it will cost about $175 for a tape deck to plug into your own TV set ... it will add only 25 per cent to the cost of a TV receiver .... Uses are easy to imagine. Tape the best shows and play them back whenever you want. (You can stop the machine during commercials or edit them out later.) Have your wife tape the afternoon ball games for viewing when you get home .... The same home machine can be used to make your original TV shows at home – instant home movies.
>
> (Scott, 1963)

The accompanying picture for this breathless *Popular Science* article depicts a reel-to-reel videotape, which dwarfs the accompanying television set. Nonetheless, it took a further decade for a videotape recorder to emerge that used a cartridge. Leading examples included the Sears 'video cartridge recorder', or the RCA 'SelectaVision', with a 'video cassette system' that could be placed on top of a television set. Such innovations closely resembled the video recorder widely used in households for the next three decades (Berger, 1972).

Once they became affordable, video recorders became an important part of television culture. Alongside viewers' taping, replaying and swapping of videos, a 'home-video' market materialized, allowing consumers to purchase videos of their favourite television programmes and series (Maddox and Court, 1989; Moran, 2002). Thus we can observe a crossover between the television industry feeding into this home-video market, and the emergence of video as a key distribution channel for cinema and movies (previously reliant on theatrical distribution) (Wasko, 1995). The local 'video store', something we now taken for granted, became an important retail outlet and local institution, providing an alternative circuit for television materials and formation of audiences (Hill and Allen, 2004).

The videotaping of programmes catalyzed a further development in the consumption and distribution of television. Not only did the video cassette allow viewers to record and replay television programmes, it also facilitated the exchange of such copied programmes. As a 'gift' economy, this informal organization of copying was a forerunner of internet peer-to-peer filesharing networks. It also amounted to what we would now call an 'informal media' economy (Marchart, 2007), operating in the gaps where traditional media business and their distribution outlets, including retail stores, fail to meet demand. As we now realize, informal media economies can actually create value and real economic (as well as cultural) benefits (Lobato, 2010). A very interesting example is provided by transnational communities of Indian, Chinese, Iranian and many other diasporas, who are able to gain access to their favourite programmes through unofficial copies being shipped from their home countries to distributors and neighbourhood shops in their countries of migration (Mabbott-Athique, 2008; Sun, 2002).

An important parallel development to that of the video recorder occurred with camera technology. Finally, the vision of the *Popular Science* writer of the early 1960s was realized. Through the grace of portable camcorders, viewers were able to make their own video programmes. Via video playback technologies, these amateur broadcasters show their productions on a television screen. At the entry level, at least, the technical gap steadily closed between 'amateur' and 'professional'. Given sufficient training, opportunity, editing, professional formation and media literacy, a dedicated individual could gain the skills and expertise to produce reasonable-quality video.

These logics of do-it-yourself television production deepened with the arrival of digital playback formats. Initially, these took the form of DVDs (Barlow, 2005; Bennett and Brown, 2008), followed later by a range of other digital formats such as Blu-ray. Typically such formats allowed content to be played back, but proved more difficult to copy (certainly the case with video). Television recording also posed difficulties – unless recordings were first made in analogue form, using existing video recorders. True, a recording could be digitized and converted to DVD. However, this involved a lengthy process requiring specialized technology. The breakthrough in consumer usability came in the form of personal, digital video recorders. With the press of a button, personal digital video recorders allowed content to be recorded in digital form (thus minimizing loss of quality). Then content could be either 'timeshifted' (played at a later time but quite soon), played back much later or transferred to other formats and devices. The upshot was that programmes could now be easily copied in digital form, and converted to commonly used video formats on computers and portable media devices. These technical breakthroughs allowed programmes to be widely distributed on increasingly cheap storage media (CDs and DVDs), and finally, bandwidth permitting, via the internet.

As I have described them here, digital video recorders were devices that could be purchased by a consumer at an electronics store, and connected to any television set. About this time there appeared another technology that gave consumers even greater options and flexibility in deciding their choice and time of watching television programmes. This was TiVo, developed in the late 1990s. The genius of TiVo lay in its promise to solve the twin problems of contemporary television: how to scan the abundance of channels to find the desired programme; and how to make such television viewing available to watch at the time the viewer wished, rather than when it was scheduled by the broadcaster. In its early incarnations TiVo could search a wide range of channels, and then record a whole series ('season pass') as well as individual programmes. Launched in the US, an eminently multichannel environment, TiVo attracted early attention because it allowed viewers to reconfigure the possibilities of what they could watch.

For their part, broadcasters were leery of how this new wave of technology shifted control of programming into the hands of viewers. For their part, TiVo's promoters reached a set of accommodations with broadcasters. For instance, TiVo did not implement a function forcing an automatic 'skip' of advertising. The ability for viewers to opt out of advertising was something that free-to-air networks had always resisted, because it threatened to strike at the heart of their business model. As TiVo became available in other countries, it often looked more like a personal digital recorder in handcuffs. Typically the TiVo was only permitted if it operated within the broadcasters' clearly established constraints – rather than something far more radical, such as, for instance, to search all available television networks and the internet for any programme in the world of television. Early on in its introduction in Australia, for instance, TiVo could be purchased for a one-off fee of $699, giving access to eleven channels from the free-to-air channels (including high-definition services). Its main competitor, Foxtel IQ, charged $200 for the device, plus $110 per month for 110 plus channels (Clements, 2008). TiVo had entered into arrangements with one dominant set of broadcasters (free-to-air), while the other set of broadcasters (the cable-television corporation Foxtel) offered its own device. The result for viewers was a split universe of television possibilities.

TiVo was on the horns of a dilemma. Like many devices, it offered the possibility to 'disintermediate' television (that is, allow consumers to access programmes directly, without relying on a particular broadcaster), then put it back together – providing consumers with a way to take all the television they could find and make viewing sense of it. However, TiVo's backers soon realized that the existing broadcasters still wielded considerable power, with their array of licences, brands and well-known programmes and personalities – not to mention their control of broadcasting networks, billing and relationships with audiences. To understand why new technology does not by itself lead to more and better media, we need to understand more about the politics of technology in television. After all, the technology that was supposed to revolutionize television from the 1990s onwards was not the internet – it was digital television. At least that was the fervent hope of the broadcasters.

The Trials and Tribulations of Digital Television

As we discovered in Chapter 2, processes of digitalization have been key to the media and new technology in the late twentieth and early twenty-first centuries. Television enjoyed its own peculiar form of this digital adventure. The thing called digital television began to seriously eventuate in the late 1980s and early 1990s (Bell, 2007). Soon we heard that digital television would herald two marvellous things, above all. Digital television was going to be about high-resolution television, taking the viewing experience to unsurpassed heights. And digital television was all about interactivity and viewer choice. Seizing control of their television screen, viewers would be presented with options to zoom into a particular shot, choose an angle and otherwise revel in the unprecedented control they would now have over their viewing experience. As it turned out, the magic of digital television was a long time coming. When it did finally arrive, the world had moved on.

In various countries, the broadcasting industries vied for the first-mover advantage in digital television – and a war erupted about which standard would be adopted. Once again, the arcane, eye-glazing world of technical standards and engineering became the highly charged area where various interests battled over the actual forms the technology would take once implemented. At stake was who would command television in the digital age (Given, 2003). The digital television wars were not only about which companies or countries were able to secure the lucrative business of making and selling new television sets, something involving not insignificant revenues given that viewers would have to replace their old analogue television sets for dazzling new digital replacements. Lurking in the fog of promises about the breakthrough quality of high-definition and digital television was a decision that went to the heart of the future of television.

Existing free-to-air broadcasters around the world had enjoyed possession of the scarce licences to broadcast television. They were now seeking to ward off the prospect of new technology opening up their market – bringing many more competitors into their heavily regulated and protected turf. Hence the old networks tended to favour high-definition television because it would require lots of spectrum, leaving much less available to be allocated to new entrants. The converse was true of the new kids on the block – the companies keen to gain a slice of the television industry. The newbies did not want a standard to be adopted that favoured high definition if the result was only a paltry quantity of extra spectrum for their new services. Rather the potential new competitors, and their investors, exerted pressure on regulators to take the opportunity presented by digital television to free up spectrum – bearing in mind that digital technology can theoretically use spectrum more efficiently and precisely than its analogue forebears – and so allow new channels to be introduced by fresh operators. To make a long story short, the battle over digital television raged for quite some years. By the middle of the first decade of the twenty-first century, though, a rough consensus was reached around the world (Brown and Picard, 2005; Cave and Nakamura, 2006). The digital switchover was on (Starks, 2007). We were turning off the old analogue television, and booting up the digital television of the future.

Not surprisingly, the transition from analogue to digital proved more difficult and protracted than planned. The first obstacle encountered was consumer resistance and apathy at the prospect of switching to digital television. An obvious and initial problem was cost, as receivers proved quite expensive in the early years. As economies of scale and diffusion started to kick in (Rogers, 1995) and the price of digital television receivers dropped, consumers remained relatively unmoved by the mooted benefits of the new technology. The stimulation of consumer demand for digital television was not only a challenge for its purveyors, it became a problem for public policy itself. Thus government as well as industry campaigns were designed to promote digital television and public inquiries were held (US House of Representatives Standing Committee on Communications, 2006).

When government and other interests worry about consumer take-up of new technology, we see a fascinating dynamic at work. A new technology cannot speak for itself (Latour, 1996) and its potential users are not very well acquainted with how it works or feels. Short of seeing the technology in store, seeing advertisements or reading information about it, or experiencing it in a friend or family member's house, the user has scant opportunity to appreciate or foretell the advantages it might confer over the technology with which they are currently familiar. When consumers are steadfastly unmoved at the prospect of encountering a new technology, despite the provision of information and marketing, and the slow diffusion of technology in some households at least, then industry tries to redouble its efforts. When this still fails, the industry turns to other supporters – such as the state. As many governments did believe that state intervention into digital television take-up was warranted, so nationwide switch-over policies were formulated.

To be fair, the need for government action goes directly to the question of the scale, scope and system-wide nature of technology. The digital television set in one's home is only the half of it. The receiver is the tip of the iceberg, so to speak. A digital television set is connected to, and embedded in, an enormous, interdependent technology system (Hughes, 1987). Without this technological system, digital broadcasting – in its guise as the successor to television broadcasting of the twentieth century – cannot succeed. Thus once digital television was determined upon by governments and industry, with acquiescence from citizens and some nascent interest from consumers, programmes were devised to work through the complex implementation of ensuring universal coverage across different areas (dealing with transmission and reception problems, and television 'black spots'). Over some decades, expectations had grown so that it was assumed that everyone in a nation would have access to television programmes. Accordingly, in the digital switchover it was important to ensure at least equivalent coverage. In addition, particular groups of viewers needed targeted campaigns to explain how digital television would work, and what options they would have to buy sets and tune into channels.

One group that had not been very well served by traditional broadcasting that became more visible in the transition to digital television were consumers with disabilities. Closed captioning of programmes for deaf people and those with hearing impairments had become standard across many countries in the 1990s (Downey, 2008; US House of Representatives, 1984). The idea was that recorded and live programmes would carry captions in order that people could read these via specialized receivers to understand what was going on. Closed captions differ from open captions, which can be read without the need for particular equipment. Of course, open captions allow themselves to be read by other viewers who might be in a poor noise environment, or wish to follow the text as well as sound and dialogue. There is a relationship between subtitling different languages, now very common on DVDs (as well as in television and movies) and closed and open captioning. Only after a considerable struggle did closed captioning become a standard entitlement in digital television for deaf people (Goggin and Newell, 2003). This is an irony given the fact that digital television was billed as a marvellous new technology. A further irony is that the convergence of text with television has had a relatively long history, as demonstrated by the precursor of Teletext. If text on television for deaf people and those with hearing disabilities was a hard-won achievement, a greater struggle still ensued over audio description for blind people. Whereas blind or partially sighted people can follow dialogue, narration and sound on television, images are difficult or impossible for many to detect (Smith, 2010). Hence the idea of describing the scene or images emerged, and the need to weave this description of the vision into the other sound and dialogue (Genensky *et al.*, 1968). Like closed captioning, the advent of digital technology in television offered many more options for how audio description could be realized, and an expanded range of viewer choices (Simpson, 1999). Audio description remains a work in progress in digital television, as in other media.

As well as provoking a focus on those viewing, listening and consuming television, the switchover saw digital television take centre stage in media reform for another reason: spectrum. When digital television was finally introduced around the world it did free up precious spectrum. Due to the precision of which it was capable, there was no need to set aside neighbouring frequencies to ensure interference-free transmission. As I have mentioned, existing versus potentially new broadcasters were lining up to vie with each other for the vacated spectrum. By 2009–10 it was evident that there was an historical opportunity for spectrum to be made available, for a rich range of potential uses and users far beyond those of existing broadcasting services. This scenario was dubbed the 'digital dividend'. With mobile and wireless technologies continuing to develop on a grand scale, these industries put pressure on governments and regulators to set aside spectrum for fourth-generation (4G) networks.

The debate on digital television served to open up a much larger and more significant conversation regarding new technology and media. At stake for societies were potent, overarching questions about how to organize the development of previously distinct broadcasting, telecommunications, mobiles and computer and internet networks – all now underpinned by key, scarce resources such as spectrum. With commentators proclaiming the end of scarcity (Bell, 1999) as the guiding principle of the media economy, and emphasizing that excess was now the problematic to address (Sawhney, 2010), the irony is that it turns out, after all, that scarcity still does endure – when it comes to sharing the radio waves (not to mention, questions of the ecological sustainability of media). A good example of the media policy-making at the digital television crossroads can be seen in the British government report *Digital Britain*. Here the British government takes the opportunity of the digital-television dividend to propose various options for the future of broadcasting, and indeed media and communications in general:

> Digital Britain primarily seeks to position the UK as a long-term leader in communications, creating an industrial framework that will fully harness Digital Technology. The UK's digital dividend will transform the way business operates, enhance the delivery of public services, stimulate communications infrastructure ready for next-generation distribution and preserve Britain's status as a global hub for media and entertainment. Most importantly of all this approach seeks to maximise the digital opportunities for all of us, as citizens, where access to 21st Century technologies will be a key competitive advantage for generations to come.
>
> (Department for Business, 2009)

One interesting place where digital television and telecommunications networks converged was mobile television. The idea of mobile television was that television could be broadcast directly to mobile phones. The advantage of mobile television was that, using similar technology, broadcasters could find a way to beam their programmes into the device that most consumers carried with them wherever they went – the mobile phone. Dedicated standards were devised for mobile television as part of the digital-television standards developed around the world – notably the European DVB-H (digital video broadcasting – hand-held) standard (Furht and Ahson, 2008; Goggin, 2011b; Penttinen, 2009). While mobile-television trials were conducted from 2003 onwards, its introduction shortly afterwards did not go as well as expected. There was some consumer interest and innovative content and programme development (Marcus, Cereijo Roibas and Sala, 2010) but much initial mobile television had to rely upon the cellular mobile network itself – rather than the terrestrial television broadcasting network – to send content to phones. This was because dedicated spectrum for mobile-television broadcasting was slow to eventuate (Goggin, 2011b). The slow growth of mobile-television also had to do with other trajectories in the field of new technologies and the media – many of which, as we shall see, blindsided the digital-television acolytes.

As we have seen, the brave new technology of digital television unfolded quite differently than expected. In the meantime, it was the relatively well-established technology of cable television that consolidated itself – then made the running, and changed the shape of television. Delivery of television by cable or wired network dates back to the late 1920s. In Britain, a company calling its Broadcast Relay set-up one of the world's first cable-distribution systems, broadcast audio signals via a wired network (Clode, 2010b). Forming the company Rediffusion in 1931, it later re-broadcast or relayed television, something known as 'Piped TV' – and by 1963 claimed 1 million subscribers worldwide (Clode, 2010a). The first cable network in North America was launched in the 1950s (Patrick, 2008). By the early 1970s, cable networks were being acclaimed and imagined as revolutionary in terms akin to those used about the information superhighway in the early to mid-1990s (Kyrish, 1994), or indeed the purple prose in which Web 2.0, social media and so on are avidly discussed today.

Cable networks were thought to hold great promise for citizen feedback, participation and public access to media (Hollander, 1985; Pool, 1973; Price and Wicklein, 1972). Cable television was hailed as a 'new era', credited with introducing competition and consumer choice into broadcasting environments dominated by free-to-air television networks – and in so doing fundamentally changing the economic possibilities of the medium (Veljanovski and Bishop, 1983). Cable television also helped to bring new cultural material from foreign countries into markets where existing licensed television stations had historically or culturally preferred domestic or regional material, or imported and adapted shows from other countries. Specifically much US audiovisual content – including famous soap operas and dramas, and other entertainment and news – could be carried on cable television because of a combination of factors: the extra channel capacity (requiring additional programmes to fill the space); the entrance of new broadcasters in television provision; and a distinct orientation on the part of many cable-television companies towards targeting the new and unmet cultural aspirations and preferences of viewers. Cable television became associated with global media franchises and brands such as the US CNN, which offered twenty-four-hour news around the world. With cable television came the concept of 'multichannel' television (Mullen, 2008; Setzer and Levy, 1991). Interestingly, an industry journal called *Multichannel News* was set up in 1980, and continues today also at multichannel.com, focusing now on the many other new media 'channels' available. As it turned out, cable television did provide new capacity for additional programming, greater media diversity and a means of addressing other perceived social, cultural and political problems associated with television. Yet in many jurisdictions around the world, the arrangements that evolved for this new technology brought all-too-familiar problems, requiring new policy and regulatory responses.

A key issue in ensuring real competition in cable television revolved around traditional issues of political economy and ownership and control of both content and carriage (Wasko, 1995). In cable television, there was quite a complicated ecology of programmes, companies packaging and distributing these, cable systems operators and those controlling the various aspects of intermediate technology (crucially, the electronic programme guides). In the US, for instance, two influential groups were: suppliers of programming to cable television, such as CNN, HBO, Discovery, Disney and ESPN; and the cable-television systems operators Time Warner and TCI. There was the problem of vertical integration; for example, operators acquiring interests in programming, represented in the Time Warner–Turner Broadcasting merger. Turner made its name with CNN, and now owns Cartoon Network and TBS, the latter known for its comedies such as *Family Guy* (1999–) and *The Office* (2005–). Add to all this the problem of horizontal integration, especially in the realm of the television systems operators – where mergers meant the great concentration of ownership and control in the critical 'bottle-neck' infrastructure of cable networks (Waterman and Weiss, 1997). To explain: cable networks involve placing cable in conduits underground, or carrying them on electricity poles, in order to create an infrastructure for household connection. Clearly it is expensive to lay and connect cable, so there is considerable 'sunk' investment already made by cable-television operators. Such a barrier to provision of new infrastructure can be overcome with satellite technology, hence the multichannel television offered to households in many developing countries via this means. Here the principal expense in broadcasting transmission lies in securing satellite transponder space and capacity (on the operator's side), and in the cost of the satellite disk, decoder and fit-out of equipment (on the household's side). Hence in principle there is a lower barrier to entry than in cable television networks *per se*.

In this new politics of multichannel broadcasting, cable television provides programmes to audiences previously not well served, not well defined and little differentiated by broadcast television: gay and lesbian audiences; particular ethnoracial groups, such as African-American audiences in the US; taste communities, such as those interested in cooking programmes, or cult series such as *The West Wing* (1999–2006), *The Wire* (2002–8), or *Mad Men* (2007–) (Banet-Weiser, Chris and Freitas, 2007). New regional media corporations, and cultural forms were also created through cable television, with power blocs being established in the former periphery countries, which then were able to sell their programmes to the countries that had been the centre of broadcasting power, such as the US and Europe. Thus cable television was deeply involved in changing patterns of migration, trade, sociodemographics and geopolitics (Sinclair, Jacka and Cunningham, 1995). A good example lies in the *telenovela*, the soap-opera form developed in Latin America (Lopez-Pumarejo, 1987; Mazziotti, 2006). The *telenovela* has not only proved popular and socially potent among Latin-American audiences (Vink, 1998) but has also been avidly watched by immigrant, binational populations of North America and elsewhere. Building on bases in Brazil, Mexico and elsewhere, the *telenovela* has also allowed media giants in Latin America to gain global reach and revenue (Sinclair, 1999), and it has influenced other forms of television soap opera and drama.

The entrenchment of multichannel television led to many debates about its cultural implications and politics. Did the 'narrow-casting' enabled by the formations of this new media technology mean an end to the cross-societal 'water-cooler' conversations and 'imagined' national communities (Anderson, 2006)? Or did cable television catalyze new kinds of public spheres, tied to distinct modes of cultural citizenship and consumer identity? These are questions we encounter once more when the twin powers of cable and broadcast television – and their home-video and DVD box-set affiliates – are infiltrated and confronted by something 'beyond' broadcasting (Hollins, 1984; Meikle and Young, 2007; Miller and Allen, 1995), something talked about as 'post'-broadcasting (Miller and Allen, 1995; Turner and Tay, 2009). What these terms refer to is the unfolding of a new 'post-network' era (Lotz, 2009) in which television networks as we have known them have lost their dominance, and are forced to regroup in order to think hard about their ultimate rationale.

Internet Audiences Overcoming Television

So far my discussion of broadcasting media has traced the contours of the technologies themselves, following something of a technical template. However, there are other developments occurring alongside of – and indeed threaded through – these technologies. The 1990s and the first decade of the twenty-first century witnessed highly significant changes in television. The antecedents and histories of these transformations stretch well beyond into earlier media forms, but it is in the mid-to-late 1990s in particular, that we see all manner of developments in television programmes, formats and audiences, associated with new technologies. Notable elements include: the rise of new kinds of interactivity associated with 'reality' and 'participation' television formats; the growth of entertainment programmes (such as lifestyle programmes); the broadening of traditional news to include the private and personal sphere (as already seen with blogs, Twitter and social media); and many people relying on comedy and satirical forms for news and current affairs. The internet has amplified many of these changes to television, and added other important dynamics.

At least since the mid-1990s an idea had taken hold that media convergence was something that television's purveyors needed to take into consideration – especially in relation to the internet (Owen, 1999). Despite this, few anticipated, yet alone grasped, the scale, direction and velocity of change the internet did bring when it finally arrived in the world of television (Crandall, 2005; Nuechterlein and Weiser, 2005). This may have been due to the slowness of the internet in establishing sufficient bandwidth, applications and user cultures to achieve the kind of platform needed for a wide-scale intervention and interaction with television. Such difficulties can be observed in the discussion in a thoughtful 2004 collection on *Internet Television*:

Internet television is the quintessential digital convergence medium, putting together television, telecommunications, the Internet, computer applications, games, and more. It is part of a historic move from individualized narrowband capacity, measured by kilobits per user, to one of broadband with a capacity of megabits per user. This move will have major consequences for many aspects of society and the economy, similar to the impact the automobile had when it replaced trains, horses, and bicycles. It will affect, in particular, the medium now called television.

(Gerbarg and Noam, 2004)

The editors predicted that:

This new medium is knocking at the door. Already, music is reaching millions of listeners around the world through the internet. Video clips have traveled likewise. It will not be long before popular video programs are regularly delivered over the Internet as well, at significantly better quality and lower cost.

(Gerbarg and Noam, 2004)

In 2004, the varieties of internet television identified in this book were still in their relative infancy. This is also the case with the key technology of peer-to-peer filesharing. P2P had made considerable inroads into media industries with the great popularity of Napster in the realm of music, yet bandwidth remained a stumbling block for video:

Attracting more recent attention than any other attribute of the Internet is the remarkable ease with which content, including movies or other videos, can be duplicated and transferred from one consumer to another. The popularity of Napster and gnutella-like file sharing systems has been a testament to these efficiencies. The limited use with video content on these systems thus far is no doubt due largely to bandwidth constraints ... .

(Waterman, 2004)

In the meantime, tried-and-tested alternative channels had to suffice.

Video-on-demand, for instance, had been discussed for quite some time (Beros, 2004; Koch, 1998; Minoli, 1995). The basic idea was that a viewer would be able to select a desired title through their telecommunications or internet provider, and have it instantaneously delivered, rather than needing to hire a video from the local store. However, 'video dial-tone', or the idea that one could order a video as easily as picking up a phone, has been slow to become commercially feasible. Video-on-demand was amended to 'near' video-on-demand, as it proved difficult to implement a sufficiently fast service. Indeed telecommunications and pay-television companies faced with the difficulties of engineering networks for video distribution resorted for some years to running mail-order video and DVD outfits with only the ordering of the title completed online – otherwise DVDs would be mailed out to customers, who would watch them and mail them back when finished.

From 2005, we can see the internet and television evolving much more closely – what we could call a 'co-evolution'. Broadband networks had become reasonably ubiquitous in many countries and better-off communities around the world. There was a better infrastructure underpinning the internet, and thus better support for the distribution of video. Actually the core of the network had high capacity for some time (typically with optical fibre in the 'backbone' or 'long-haul' links). The remaining challenge lay in the 'last mile' of the networks underpinning the internet. That is, the question exercising minds was how to extend broadband transmission capacity to the edges of the network – to the the households themselves and the fast-proliferating devices now resident in users' everyday environments. There was also the now closely related question of how to extend good bandwidth to the user through wireless and mobile networks (evident in mobile broadband technology, discussed in Chapter 2). In any case, infrastructure had improved to the extent that the long-lived video store and mail-order model was able to be seriously challenged by organizations such as Netflix in the US, which allowed movies and TV to be streamed to an available device in the household (including Microsoft's Xbox 360). Already by 2009, Netflix offered an estimated 10 million titles (Merrill Lynch, 2009), and its nascent role was being challenged by other distribution channels such as Apple's iTunes. Hand in hand with the evolution of bandwidth were the rich, new possibilities of internet applications and cultures themselves.

P2P applications for video-file transfer were developed at the turn of the twentieth century, with the notorious BitTorrent initially released in 2001. The idea of such clients is that they create a network of 'peers', allowing each user to upload and download material. The genius of P2P networks lay in the fact that the protocol and application allowed the typical video file (600 megabytes – 4 gigabytes, depending on quality, length and format) to be exchanged in quite small pieces from one user (or peer) to many others, without requiring a central distribution node.

The availability of BitTorrent and similar clients led to the phenomenon of widespread sharing of television, film and video content – on a scale and type hitherto seen with Napster and music-based P2P networks. Critical to the broadening of the base of users was the establishment and visibility of 'tracker' sites. Tracker sites store torrent files, that once downloaded can activate the downloading of content from individual peer users. The most famous of these trackers has been the Swedish-initiated site *Pirate Bay* (http://thepiratebay.org/). In late 2010, *Pirate Bay* described itself as follows:

> The members at The Pirate Bay represent a broad spectrum of file sharers ... . Do not contact us if there is anything you find offensive, instead focus on the material that you find positive ... . Only torrent files are saved at the server. That means no copyrighted and/or illegal material are [sic] stored by us. It is therefore not possible to hold the people behind The Pirate Bay responsible for the material that is being spread using the tracker. Any complaints from copyright and/or lobby organizations will be ridiculed and published at the site.

Like all new technologies, in point of fact there was a fascinating precedent for P2P networks such as Napster and BitTorrent. This was the application Hotline, devised by a teenager, and released in 1996. With a largely underground following, Hotline boasted illicit, unauthorized transfer of files (pictures, movies, software and keys to provide software licences). However, Hotline never achieved a breakthrough mass following, let alone any modicum of respectability, and so it was the advent of Napster and BitTorrent, and the massive, global sharing of movies and music that led to the popular culture of downloading of television content over the internet.

With internet downloading of television programmes, aficionados of hit series – such as the US-produced *Lost* (2004–10), *The Sopranos* (1999–2007), *Six Feet Under* (2001–5), *House* (2004–) could enjoy well-developed fan sites, discussions and fan-created content. The internet was already well established as a key medium for distributing such material, and creating and sustaining audiences and viewer communities around a common interest and identification with a programme (Baym, 2000; Bury, 2005; Jenkins, 2006). It has been argued that, with internet downloading, these fan cultures – and the formation of 'cult' TV – were greatly broadened to make such kind of intense user participation a mainstream phenomenon (Ross, 2008). The process required a modicum of technical expertise and digital literacy, well within the capability of many members of audiences around the world. Viewers would digitally record a programme from television, often editing out the advertisements and adding titles or even commentary. The recording would then be encoded, prepared for use with a BitTorrent application and information about the file uploaded to a tracker site for those interested (Zuchetti, 2006).

A lot of the fun in TV downloading practices lay in gaining an (unauthorized) advance screening of episodes of a much-loved programme, especially in countries where a programme would be released a long time after its first screening in its country of origin. As one frustrated viewer opined in an Australian study:

> I want to be able to see new episodes as soon as possible so that I can discuss them with friends online in other countries. That's a big part of why I watch – it's a shared experience. It's ridiculous how long we are kept waiting for new episodes of foreign shows in this country, as though technology is the same as it was twenty or thirty years ago and we have no other choice.
>
> (Female, 26–40 years, quoted in Zuchetti, 2006)

As well as 'spoilers' for fans wishing to see the latest show as soon as possible, downloading attracted many other viewers. These downloaders included those who wished to watch shows, but had missed them or not recorded them, or who were interested in watching shows not currently available through their television networks. Soon whole series were available for download by unofficial means. In 2012, for example, the hypothetical downloader can visit Pirate Bay and find over 100 television series. Such sites are only one component of a veritable user-built archive of television series, although some downloads are of uneven quality. Nonetheless internet P2P downloading quickly began to compete with other forms of 'rerun' television. As Derek Kompare recounts, the repetition of television shows was well underway in the 1950s in the US, and 'by the early 1960s, reruns were established as an everyday part of the television schedule on local stations nationwide' (Kompare, 2005). Repeat programming was taken to new levels of intensity by cable networks in the 1980s, which developed many specialized channels that used such content (Kompare, 2005). With the popularity of the DVD player, box sets of whole series were available for purchase (Kompare, 2005; McDonald, 2007). The phenomenon of internet downloading added further support to the idea of reruns and watching whole series in a curated set in a concentrated period of time.

Alarmed by internet downloading of television, networks around the world responded by ensuring some of their programmes were available to download. This was the beginning of what is now called 'catch-up' television. The repetition of programmes shortly after they were broadcast – for example, later in the day, or later in the week – had long been a feature of television. So too had the practice of repeating programmes on another channel, especially on multichannel subscription television. With catch-up television, networks initially used their own websites to make programmes available for viewing within a set period of time (typically two to three weeks after the first broadcast).

One of the first broadcasters to launch such a service was the BBC with its dedicated iPlayer, which allows a wide range of programmes to be watched in a web browser at the viewer's convenience. The BBC also allows viewers to watch its channels broadcast live online. However, restrictions apply, meaning that viewers can usually only watch such 'catch-up' TV on the internet while in their own country. American programmes on TV network websites are generally not yet available for viewers in other countries. The same applies to BBC programmes, not least because UK citizens have long been required to pay for a licence to watch TV. Hence the error message I encountered when trying to access BBC programmes from outside the country:

> Don't forget – to watch TV online as it's being broadcast, you still need a TV Licence ... . Everyone in the UK who watches or records TV as it is broadcast needs to be covered by a TV licence. This includes TV on computers, mobile phones, DVD/video recorders and other devices.
>
> (http://www.bbc.co.uk/aboutthebbc/licencefee/)

Around the world, similar national restrictions apply to the broadcast and distribution of television material via the internet – often revealed when one travels abroad and tries to catch up with favourite programmes from home, and cannot do so.

Television broadcasters also use their websites for two other purposes than catch-up television: time-limited previews and debuts of new shows; or extra material that is only available on the internet, and will not be broadcast (rather like the custom-made extra material, outtakes, interviews and extra information available on DVDs). Both internet downloading of programmes and broadcaster responses (via their websites, catch-up portals, mobile-designed content) compete with a range of other transmission and viewing channels now. For instance,

Rush, a popular police drama on the commercial Australian television Channel 10, in late 2010 could be watched for three weeks to a month after initial broadcast via the programme's website. However, each hour-long episode comprised five to six concatenated files that had to be sequentially loaded, causing an advertisement to be played each time, as well as an interruption to viewing. The alternative offered by Channel 10 was to purchase the programme in higher resolution and uninterrupted form from Apple iTunes. Of course, this still left the unauthorized alternative: namely, to search for the latest episode on Pirate Bay, or another BitTorent site, and take one's chances with availability and quality by downloading it.

Connected, Social Television

The internet has steadily gained momentum so that it is now central to how television audiences develop and access programmes. In turn, peer-to-peer sharing of programme files has become indispensable to the actual distribution and viewing of television itself. At about the same time, there has been an important development that has helped to further displace the 'official'-version television represented by broadcaster networks.

The new internet-based architecture of video-sharing applications has provided a way that you, as the viewer, can 'broadcast yourself' (as the motto of YouTube goes). These video-sharing sites have created new forms of do-it-yourself video, genres and even, one might argue, television that can garner very large audiences. Launched in early 2005, the wildly popular YouTube describes itself as:

> the world's most popular online video community, allowing millions of people to discover, watch and share originally created videos. YouTube provides a forum for people to connect, inform, and inspire others across the globe and acts as a distribution platform for original content creators and advertisers large and small.
>
> (http://www.youtube.com/t/about)

YouTube allows anyone with an account to upload videos. As well as uploading individual videos, one can gather these into one's own 'channel' on YouTube. These are typically restricted in length, so short videos of relatively low resolution predominate. This kind of short video is also easily captured, using a wide range of consumer devices to be found in increasingly digitally saturated households, from digital cameras, dedicated video devices such as the popular Flip device, through to cameras mounted on computers and laptops, mobile-phone cameras and tablets with video, and recording and editing software on home computers. Parody and satire are prevalent in the creative, energetic vein of content available via YouTube, which draws heavily on the resources of 'mash-up' culture. Do-it-yourself, amateur and pro-am content has found a home, and jump-started the careers of YouTube users, fuelling a new phenomenon in celebrity culture. In addition, YouTube has become a repository for many pieces of 'must-watch' video, often recorded from television). Thus YouTube constitutes a handy archive of public and popular memory. There is a fair chance that videos of breaking news, events or scandals can be immediately watched on YouTube, if one has missed them on television.

At the very least, YouTube has become integrated with viewer practices of watching and consuming television, in the ways described. It has also allowed users themselves to create programmes that can be broadcast to others, via the YouTube platform. In these ways, YouTube has reworked video and television cultures, and, in doing so, shown their enduring appeal at the same time. It comes as no surprise, then, that the powerful corporate interests dominating the political economy of convergent media interests eyed YouTube as a potential threat that they needed to annex. Thus YouTube was acquired by Google in 2006 content deals were struck with leading broadcasters including CBS, the BBC, Universal Music and others. These tie-ins not only assist YouTube in gaining advertisers, but also allow it to host music videos by popular artists. The next wave of design and investment by YouTube and its backers has involved ensuring the site is easily accessible across the range of platforms available to users. Thus users can access YouTube on their phone, integrate it into their website or connect with a Facebook account or other social-media application. And YouTube has come full circle – now a natural part of what you watch on your own TV:

YouTube in Your Living Room
Dim the lights, sit back and pass the popcorn. Browse over to a special version of the YouTube website that makes it easy to watch and share your favourite YouTube videos with the whole family.
(http://www.youtube.com/youtubeonyourtv)

YouTube is the best known among a widening range of video-sharing sites and communities. It has a particular focus on harvesting and catalyzing participatory internet culture. Another more mainstream site is Hulu, which styles itself as: 'TV. Your Way. Finally, TV on your terms. Watch your favourite videos right from your browser, any time, for free' (http://www.hulu.com/about/product_tour). Videos on Hulu can be watched for free although access at time of writing was restricted to the US, unless one is able to find a work-around using Virtual Private Network software. Alternatively, by paying a fee a user can subscribe to an account for extra features, such as access to one's own video 'queue' (something familiar from mail-order video stores) – what is called the 'freemium' (or 'free/premium') model:

> *Hulu Plus. More TV. On more devices*
> Enjoy the full current season of popular shows any time. Hulu Plus gives you exclusive access to every episode, all season long, of *Glee*, *Modern Family*, *House*, and dozens of other popular shows ... from ABC, Fox, NBC, and more.
>
> Watch on your TV, mobile device, or computer. Stream episodes instantly in HD (720p) to your connected TV, Blu-ray player, gaming console, set-top box, iPad, iPhone, and other device.
>
> (http://www.hulu.com/plus)

Hulu is a good example of the vision that animates companies seeking to use the internet as a distribution, storage and viewing medium to reconfigure the boundaries of what has been regarded, respectively, as inside and outside the televisual box. Finally Hulu and other media-technology companies can deliver the long-awaited consumer revolution: now, the story goes, the viewer can watch as much TV, wherever they like, on whatever device they care for, whenever they wish to do so, with as much control and navigability over playback and interactivity as can be mustered. Or so they say. Yet for all of Hulu's self-promotion, the role of existing broadcasters and brands is still very strong. We might be watching TV on our iPad, phone or laptop, as much as via our set-top box, digital TV and media centre, yet the popular shows are more often than not the programmes we know and fondly cherish, conceived and delivered courtesy of the networks we grew up with.

The response of TV equipment manufacturers especially has been to capitalize on these commercial and popular developments with something called 'connected TV'. Connected TV implies the convergence between familiar ideas of TV (TV sets, set-top boxes, programme guides) and the internet. The idea of connected TV is that our favourite box should be connected to the internet. Connected TV is sometimes referred to as 'smart TV', reminiscent of various other 'smart' or 'intelligent' technology (not least the current vogue for 'smartphones'). As the Intel Corporation puts it:

> TV just got smarter. The Intel® Atom™ processor has intelligence and performance that powers smart TV experiences. Everything people love about TV and the internet is now together on one screen. Instantly find and watch favourite shows and movies, easily surf between channels and Web sites, and interact with TV like never before.
>
> (Intel, 2010)

As computing, internet, television and media industries try to catch the wave of internet–television convergence, there is an intriguing and potentially more radical notion afoot still: social television. Like the concept of social media, this term has an odd ring. After all, have not media been closely associated with, and indeed central to production, of the social, since their inception, as I have suggested in Chapter 1? Presumably the purpose of labelling television as 'social' at this historical moment is to take advantage of the vogue for social media. The term social television seems to have been coined in 2007 (Ducheneaut, Oehlberg, Moore, *et al.*, 2008; Schatz, Wagner, Egger, *et al.*, 2007). Social TV refers especially to the social activities that occur in and around television watching – the social practices associated with television that media ethnographers have highlighted for at least three decades (Lull, 1990; Morley, 1980). However, social TV takes this one step further, implying that these kinds of activities actually frame and construct TV itself. Those advocating social television emphasize that television is embedded in flows of social-networking systems, as well as ubiquitous and pervasive computing and mobile media. The active audience of 'produsers' not only share the texts, images, sounds, words, narratives and interpretations of television, but, decisively, engage in peer-to-peer networking of television itself:

> Sitting on the train on a rainy Monday night, after a long day at work, you have a look on your smartphone to see what's on television. Your TV operator's app thinks you might enjoy *The Big Lebowski*. After all your best mate has 'liked' it on Facebook. And it's on TV right now. A big fan of the Dude you whip out your iPad and start watching, swapping favourite quotes with your mate who you have invited to watch it with you through a chat window on your smartphone.
>
> (Graham, 2011)

So, the audience of social TV creates, edits, recommends and distributes content as much as it simply watches TV.

In mid-2010, social television was nominated by *MIT Technology Review* as one of the top ten most important emerging technology trends:

> The viewership for live television broadcasts has generally been declining for years. But something surprising is happening: events such as the Winter Olympics and the Grammys are drawing more viewers and more buzz. The rebound is happening at least in part because of new viewing habits: while people watch, they are using smart phones or laptops to swap texts, Tweets, and status updates about celebrities, characters, and even commercials.
>
> (Bulkeley, 2010)

As illustrated here, what the discourse of social television hangs on is the reliance on friendship groups and social networks in the very definition of TV. Television now exists in a world of apparent media abundance, with networks struggling to cope with the decentring of the former systems of distribution and regimes of programming. Many users are mightily dissatisfied with the still-restricted palettes and options for programme choice, and they are all too pleased to fill the breach with recommendations, ratings and adroit harnessing of the various 'like' functions of social-networking systems that rapidly circulate preferences and contribute to taste judgements. If social media is the centre of people's cultural universes, especially of young viewers, advocates suggest television should position itself squarely in the midst of social media – to find new, compelling ways to enable such sharing of information and collaboration around viewing:

> Carriers, networks, and content producers hope that making it easier for viewers to link up with friends will help them hold on to their audiences rather than losing them to services like Hulu, which stream shows over the internet. And opening TV to social networking could make it easier for companies to provide personalized programming.
>
> (Bulkeley, 2010)

The notion of social television has not set the world of media alight the way social media certainly has. However, what it tries to do is illuminating. Social television implies that companies need to focus upon, design and invest heavily in systems that support the kinds of linkages and 'sharing' between television and other media platforms. A deceptively simple task, of course, when much of this trajectory of convergence is already well underway with the welter of devices, players, business models and standards (Lampland and Star, 2009) already established in the marketplace, entailing considerable sunk investment. Further still, the problem really is as much about divergence and lack of compatibility, as it is about convergence. Take, for instance, the rubric of the relevant LinkedIn group: 'social television – next-generation media (Web 2.0, mobile, digital video broadcast, DTV, STB, MHEG, IPTV.' In effect, social television functions as an enabling fiction for what television, and indeed media itself, is failing to achieve. Social television is the dream that all parts of the convergent media puzzle might connect with each other; or at least come together as particular forces and actors in new media and technology would like. In this scenario, the viewer is back with a vengeance, but is saddled with quite a bit of work: creating their own, personal television, as well as helping their friends, family and associates to do the same, whizzing across platforms, new media cultures, time and space.

If social television is a project about as fuzzy as social media itself – and one in which corporate interests of various sorts are in the vanguard of shaping – the biggest change to television looks set to come from another direction: the promises and politics of next-generation networks. As explored in Chapter 2, serious investment around the world is being ploughed into next-generation broadband networks that promise 100 megabits per second (Mbps), or more, as standard. In many cases these next-generation networks are premised on the extension of optical fibre from the core of the network to the household itself. There is a long way to go before such visions are comprehensively and ubiquitously realized – though countries like South Korea, Singapore and Japan were already well down this track at least a decade before others thought it necessary. With the kinds of speeds and data capacity promised, the great barrier to video distribution will be finally lowered. Therefore, the next-generation broadband networks genuinely stand to become alternatives to existing cable, terrestrial and satellite broadcasting.

In a number of countries, the long-established development path upgrading to digital-television transmission is seriously questioned by the soon-to-be-viable option of broadcasting television programmes to consumers via next-generation broadband networks. IP TV – the broadcasting of television via internet networks – is now very well placed to become a very popular way to access television, overcoming the

constraints of bandwidth, quality and scalability of network infrastructure thus far. In addition, cable-television providers are well placed to
use new broadband networks for delivery, if they can strike the right
deals to migrate their content from the old cable networks (Merrill
Lynch, 2009). It is the great survivors of television that face the greatest
challenge: the free-to-air terrestrial networks. Their transmission model
uses the airwaves to beam television to viewers' sets – a long-standing
arrangement which they hoped to upgrade through the transition to
digital television (Alcatel-Lucent, 2009; Bartholomeusz, 2009). The
appearance of fully fledged next-generation networks that can push TV
down the pipes, making internet TV a reality is a very scary prospect
indeed. There stands to be a genuine alternative rising from the mess of
networks that comprise internet infrastructure. If it can broadcast digital television with the same quality and resolution as the broadcasting
infrastructure, will consumers finally turn off the traditional TV? After
all, they will be promised all that television represents, plus the cornu-
copia of the internet too.

The Very Idea of Television

New technology has been a constant in the history and development of
television, as we have seen. Since the early 1990s there have been
steadily louder predictions that technology will change the face of television. Dramatic changes have indeed eventuated – to the programmes
that are shown on television; to the facts of how, where and why viewers watch them; to the kinds of practices audiences engage in; and to
the ways in which television fits in with other forms of media and
culture. Multichannel television has become a reality for many viewers
around the world. Television is embedded in the internet. Yet the stuff
that formerly belonged on the box is now avidly watched on many
more kinds of personal, portable media devices than were previously
imaginable. While the average amount of hours of television watched
may have slightly dropped in recent surveys, in favour of the internet,
the medium is still well entrenched and highly popular. Indeed, we are
not entirely sure how much of the time people spend using the internet
now is actually to consume content that they would have previously
found on traditional TV. What is abundantly clear is that, like with the
press, predictions of television's demise are exaggerated.

Also fanciful are the claims that digital technology has revolutionized
television. The broadcasters and equipment manufacturers circulated

version 1.0 of this myth, with their keen desire to gain acceptance for the introduction of digital terrestrial television. But perhaps this simply resulted in the broadcasters over-thinking about how television could be something other or more.* The resurgence in television highlighted by the 2010 annual survey in the *Economist* can be read as due to broadcasters and a range of new media players figuring out how to use other media tools to add value to the live experience (noting that Twitter feeds are not as compelling if you are watching TV on delay). Over the longer term, television's recapturing of ground has been partly about raising the standard of one of the things the medium does best – shows with high production value. Moreover, these expensive, richly designed and plotted shows, like the US series *Mad Men* or UK series *Downton Abbey* (2010–), take television further into the realm of cultural forms such as cinema and the novel.

Version 2.0 of the myth is that, digital television having proved relatively prosaic, a revolution has occurred in the relations among television's producers, broadcasters and viewers. It is now commonplace for audiences to be not only active, but, in the land of connected TV, actually calling the shots. We need to be very careful about assuming that television has been revolutionized (to invert the title of Gil Scott-Heron's 1970 song). As Amanda D. Lotz points out:

> Viewers have come to enjoy a meaningful increase in and expanded diversity of programming as a result of the industrial changes of the multichannel transition and emerging post-network era, and television has come to be revolutionized in comparison with network-era norms. However, commercial interests still control production, and viewers' choice is still limited as there remains much that cannot be found on television. The new possibilities in programming that have been achieved are significant, but by no means do they indicate that viewers now control the process or that a democratization of the medium has occurred.
>
> (Lotz, 2007, pp. 254–5)

That users now control television is just another myth about new technology and the media. As with the other myths considered in this book, a sceptical approach is required. The critical approach recommended throughout this book offers handsome dividends in the case of television

---

* My thanks to Jock Given for this point.

also. Many of the things attributed to the current wave of new technologies affecting television have been heralded in earlier epochs, often in surprisingly similar terms – whether videotaping, cable television, digital television or early forms of internet. As always, it is important to cultivate a historical sense of the construction of new technology. Also we once again need to undertake a close examination and analysis of what exactly is happening with the new technology as it interacts with television. What are the technical characteristics of new technology? What affordances and possibilities do the technologies hold (that is, what are their capabilities, according to their designers and promoters, and what more could we actually do with them, if we desired)? Which actors and interests are influential in shaping the future of television through controlling new technology? What is the evidence for claims being made about how television, and media generally, might be arranged? What new kinds of audiences and cultural practices are emerging? How should all of these things change public discourse and the policy and research agenda on television and media generally?

5 New Associations: Technology in Media Professions and Institutions

Newspapers make associations and associations make newspapers.

Alexis de Tocqueville (cited in Rosen, 2010)

Your voice matters. Now, if you have something worth saying, you can be heard. You can make your own news. We all can.

Dan Gillmor (Gillmor, 2004, p. 241)

Broadcasting is a civic art. It is intrinsically public in ambition and effect. We may experience it individually, but it is never a purely private transaction.

British Broadcasting Corporation (BBC, 2005)

As media transformations associated with new technology have deepened since the late 1980s, there has been a growing realization that these changes have considerable implications for two strategically important areas: professions and institutions. These things are closely related and in many ways are slower to change than the other areas we have so far considered. So, what is the impact of these developments in new technologies on notions of professionalism, and on the funding and character of media institutions?

There has long been debate about the nature of professions in media, and whether it is accurate to characterize, for instance, journalism as a profession. As evident in the discussion of news and new technology in Chapter 3, notions of professionalism are also challenged by the ideas and practices associated with new technologies. This is especially the case with the figure of the user, rise of the amateur and burgeoning role of the media citizen, all now invested with great power and promise. To introduce the issues at stake in this chapter, I focus upon one especially important media profession affected by new technology: journalism. For some time, the nature of journalism has been under serious review and redefinition, the economic bases of journalism as a profession being steadily eroded, with newspapers needing to adopt all manner of strategies to survive, whether it be the compact-format newspaper, tipping the balance in favour of entertainment rather than 'hard' news or the emergence of mobile and online news. Amid all these changes, the debates over journalism as a profession are deepening, with new contributions from educators, employers and members of society and the public all having a stake in the identity of journalism as a profession. In what follows, I look at the new alternatives to traditional professional guises, movements such as citizen or grassroots journalism (and other mobilizations of the 'people formerly known as the audience'). I also discuss countervailing responses to regain the authority and credibility of journalism as a profession such as j-blogging (blogging by journalists).

As the case of journalism reveals, concepts of professionalism also have strong links to particular kinds of media institutions. In the second part of the chapter, I look at the way that public-service broadcasters – now often called public-service media – have availed themselves of new technologies. As Andrew Crisell notes in his study of television based on the influential British case, there are two main philosophies that have shaped the heritage of public-service media. First, the contrast public-service broadcasters draw between their offerings and their perception of commercial television as 'predominantly a medium of entertainment and abbreviated news, whose products exist in a market where, in accordance with the demand for them, they are bought by viewers and/or paid by advertisers' (Crisell, 2006, pp. 170–1). Second, the 'old "public service" view that it is a common cultural resource rather like schools, libraries, museums and art galleries and spiritually analogous to universal health-care', that should be 'funded by all viewers to ensure comprehensive provision, even for certain minority tastes'(Crisell, 2006, p. 170). In recent times, however, many public-service media around the world – from Britain's BBC, through Japan's NHK to Australia's multicultural broadcaster SBS – have been pioneers in cross-platform, multimedia broadcasting, with innovative use of online media. While sometimes slow to grasp the full significance of what they were doing, the public-service media's canny appropriation of new technology has fortified and extended their mission (as well as helping them to deal with governmental and political constraints on their funding). However, such an adroit engagement with new technologies has also brought the ire of commercial media. Thus News Corporation in Britain and various actors in German debates have argued strenuously that public-service media are overreaching their traditional mission, taking advantage of public money, to compete for markets. Thus the case of public-service media illustrates the vitally important debates underway regarding the very nature of future institutions in media – in which how we understand new technology is absolutely key.

New Technology and the Fourth Estate

While journalism may, in some quarters at least, be a prestigious profession, like many others it was not so long ago held in disrepute (Cryle, 1997). For some, journalism is not so much a profession as an occupation, a form of waged work (Carr-Saunders and Wilson, 1933; Dunn, 2004; Tunstall, 1996). In addition, within the industry itself, most journalists define journalists simply as people who get paid to do journalism – and do not worry too much about the label of a 'profession'.* Further, for much time – perhaps all its short life – journalism has been widely thought to be in need of reform. The putative ills of journalism are many and various. Crucially, what ails journalism is believed to beset the health of democracy itself – so the links between media, society and power, are highly visible in these debates over its status as a profession. Into these worries about journalism as a profession enter the current ideas attaching to digital technology.

While new technology is commonly thought to be a key factor adversely affecting the profession of journalism, it was not always viewed in this way. In recent times, we can point to the advent of camera technology and satellite broadcast technology in the late 1980s and early 1990s, as a period in which there were significant transformations in how news was gathered, journalism done, media produced and how it affected the role of journalism and news in public and private spheres. However, it was the cumulative effect of these technologies with others centring on the internet that profoundly broadened the debate about journalism. Hence now new technology is widely believed, without exaggeration, to be bound up with the life and death of the profession itself. It is important to put this heightened emphasis on new technology as the engine of change in, and agent of challenge

---

* My thanks to Penny O'Donnell for these ideas, and for alerting me to the importance of continuing debates about journalism as a profession, into which new technology plays.

to, journalism in context – adding to the long-standing discussions about its status and prospects as a profession just mentioned.

As outlined in Chapter 3, journalism is part of the press. Some of the key issues and challenges faced by journalism flow from transformations and crises in the press. New technologies, especially the internet, extend the possibilities of distribution, consumption, reach and significance of the press. The press takes diverse forms in different parts of the world, so the response to new technologies is also quite particular. Journalists are trained in, educated for and work in particular parts of the press, and media generally, and their careers, especially now, unfold across quite different areas of communication. Nonetheless, the commercial press has been a central part of how journalism as a profession has evolved, affecting the identities of those who belong to it and the social functions of journalism. The migration of critical activities and revenues that the commercial press relies upon, especially advertising, to the internet has raised real questions about the financial viability of the press and the business models that underpin it. This has direct implications for how journalism is understood as a profession. To put it most dramatically, particular kinds of work that journalists undertake, that also have a privileged link to beliefs about what constitutes journalism, may no longer be possible to sustain. Thus debate rages about the profession of journalism, which I'll seek to elucidate from a critical-technology perspective.

Let me start with the broad position that new technology is changing the profession of journalism for the better. There are many scholars and commentators who can be viewed as arguing for this proposition, who come from very different traditions and standpoints and draw upon varying bases of evidence and argument to characterize the profession, its imperatives and the challenges they believe it faces. The optimistic position is associated with a diverse group of writers, activists and others who share the belief that new technology associated with the internet is making journalism much more inclusive – broadening its base beyond the profession to allow anyone – with sufficient skills, expertise and a point of view – to take advantage of the ease of access of the technology to contribute journalism-like material to old and new media organs of news.

An influential advocate of the thesis that new internet technology brings the democratization of journalism is Dan Gillmor, whose ideas are articulated in his book *We the Media: Grassroots Journalism by the People, for the People* (Gillmor, 2004, pp. 3–4). Gillmor sees the origins of journalism in pamphleteers such as Benjamin Franklin's *Pennsylvania*

Gazette and Thomas Paine's eighteenth-century writings about liberty and democracy. In the twentieth century, Gillmor discerns a shift away from the previous emphasis on 'personal journalism' and 'individuals who found ways to work outside the mainstream of the moment', towards an inevitable transition to the corporatization of journalism through the dominance of 'big business' (Gillmor, 2004, pp. 3–4). According to Gillmor, the hegemony of big business over media and news in the US reached its peak in the 1960s and 1970s and saw worthwhile achievements – notably support for nationally significant investigative reporting. However, the transfer of ownership of news networks to non-media corporations such as General Electric and the Loews Corporation, and the rise of local news stations with an emphasis on sensationalism in reporting ('if it bleeds, it leads') (Gillmor, 2004, pp. 5–6), meant that informed, serious journalism took a dive. Enter technology, and things looked up again. The technology for Gillmor that made the crucial difference was cable television, exemplified by the 'daring experiment' of CNN news, which 'punched a hole in a dam that was already beginning to crumble from within' (Gillmor, 2004, pp. 6–7). However, cable technology was still controlled by whoever owned the cables, so it was left to 'personal choice, assisted by the power of personal technology' in the form of computers and online communications to counter the forces of 'centralization and corporate ownership' (Gillmor, 2004, pp. 7–8). Gillmor mentions other important developments underpinned by new technology such as desktop publishing, talk radio and the growth of independent ethnic media. The *coup de grâce* was the World Wide Web:

> Communications had completed a transformation. The printing press and broadcasting are a one-to-many medium. The telephone is one-to-one. Now we had a medium that was anything we wanted it to be: one-to-one, one-to-many, and many-to-many. Just about anyone could own a digital printing press, and have worldwide distribution.
>
> (Gillmor, 2004, p. 13)

The entrenchment of open-source technologies and communities – manifested in the open-source news we encountered in Chapter 3 – deepened the foundations for a new kind of participatory journalism.

The potential of these new technological architectures for, and social relations of, journalism was demonstrated by the events of September 11, 2001. Here bloggers and others using the tools of the internet were able to provide information, context and images that showed that old journalism had been superseded. Gillmor terms this the 'read-write' web:

> By the turn of the new century, the key building blocks of emergent, grassroots journalism were in place. The Web was already a place where established news organizations and newcomers were plying an old trade in updated ways, but the tools were making it easier for anyone to participate. We needed a catalyst to show how far we'd come. On September 11, 2001, we got that catalyst in a terrible way.
>
> (Gillmor, 2004, p. 18)

For Gillmor, ordinary media users – at least those critically equipped members of it – had taken up the cause:

> I'm most gratified at how the 'former audience', as I call it, has taken these tools and turned its endless ideas into such unexpected, and in some cases superb, forms of journalism. Yes, this new media has created, or at least exacerbated, difficult issues of credibility and fairness. We'll be wrestling with these issues for decades, but I'm confident that the community, with the assistance of professional journalists and others who care, can sort it all out.
>
> (Gillmor, 2004, p. 238)

Interestingly here, Gillmor, a journalism academic himself, sees a key role for professional journalists – a paradox we have already encountered in the case of the South Korean OhmyNews project (Chapter 3), and which we explore further as we precede.

In his account of 'we' media, Gillmor relies upon key assumptions and points of reference. He cites with approval media theorists such as Marshall McLuhan (McLuhan, 1964, 1967) and Alvin Toffler (Toffler, 1970, 1980), as well as the contemporary and systematic account of Yochai Benkler (Benkler, 2006). Gillmor also relies upon other theorists often associated with the participatory turn in digital media. These thinkers include Howard Rheingold, with his celebrated account of 'smart mobs' (Rheingold, 2002), which inspired a great deal of other work looking at the role of text messaging and other forms of mobile messaging in the formation of new kinds of informal organizations and collective action. Of course, Gillmor's book is – like all work in the area – already dated, but it is an influential account that still clearly and engagingly illustrates the strengths and shortcomings of this 'calling into question' of journalism. It encourages us to scrutinize journalism and what it contributes to society. Gillmor also presses us to enlarge the enchanted circle of those who may contribute to journalism. Using technology as an explanatory frame, it urges action by all to enliven reporting and journalism, and to make its fruits more widely available – via the new networks and tools of such collective action. Gillmor is alive to what is emergent and distinctive about technology and its use, and indicates its potential for better journalism, and also new, stronger, more active linkages between journalists, their audiences and their spheres of action (not least democracy). However, there are significant shortcomings in Gillmor's view of journalism, which are revealing – because these are weaknesses often encountered in more rigorous versions of the position he represents. The central problem is an over-statement of the enabling possibilities of the technology, and a concomitant neglect of the institutions that mediate technology and constitute the social identities and practices that make up journalism.

Another commentator emphasizing the paradigm shift in journalism as a profession is Jay Rosen (also an American journalism professor, based at New York University). Famously, Rosen published the follow-ing fictitious manifesto on his blog:

> The people formerly known as the audience wish to inform media people of our existence, and of a shift in power that goes with the platform shift you've all heard about … . The writing readers. The viewers who picked up a camera. The formerly atomized listeners who with modest effort can connect with each other and gain the means to speak – to the world, as it were.
>
> (Rosen, 2006)

Rosen spells out the platform shift as follows:

> The people formerly known as the audience are those who *were* on the receiving end of a media system that ran one way, in a broadcasting pattern, with high entry fees and a few firms competing to speak very loudly while the rest of the population listened in isolation from one another – and who *today* are not in a situation like that *at all* … .
>
> You were once (exclusively) the editors of the news, choosing what ran on the front page. Now we can edit the news, and our choices send items to our own front pages. A highly centralized media system had connected people 'up' to big social agencies and centers of power but not 'across' to each other. Now the horizontal

flow, citizen-to-citizen, is as real and consequential as the vertical one.

(Rosen, 2006)

Elswhere Rosen develops arguments about the implications of this fundamental shift for journalism:

> We are early in the rise of semi-pro journalism, but well into the decline of an older way of life within the tribe of professional journalists ... . The land that newsroom people have been living on – also called their business model – no long supports their best work ... to keep the professional press going, the news tribe will have to migrate across the digital divide and re-settle itself on *terra nova*, new ground. Or as we sometimes call it, a new platform.

(Rosen, 2008)

Like many who broadly share his perspective Rosen draws a distinction between 'journalism' and 'media'. For Rosen, the priority task is how all of us can resuscitate, renovate and re-house the traditions of social, responsible journalism:

> in general we have no reason to trust the media to bring serious journalism across the great divide, into a new and democratic life on the Web. And so we have to do it ourselves, whatever *that* means.

(Rosen, 2005)

In a 2010 lecture to journalism students in Paris, Rosen calls for a new conception of the profession adequate to the shift underway:

> The digital revolution changes the equation ... . And so you have the opportunity to become the journalists formerly known as the media, carrier class for a new understanding of the people 'out there' on the receiving end of what journalists make. I say 'new', but it is really just another chapter in the long struggle to make good on the idea of a public that knows what is happening because it pays attention, informs itself and argues about what should be done.

(Rosen, 2010)

Gillmor and Rosen are two leading proponents of the optimistic view of the prospects for a radical change in the profession of journalism. Their positions are shared by many others, though I hasten to add that, there are many who take a less than positive view. Many aspects of their position are not actually to do with technology *per se*, but to do with what might be associated with it. Rosen, for instance, is a leading figure in 'public journalism', a movement that developed in the 1990s to advocate for the capacity of journalism to make a better contribution to the quality of public life (Glasser, 1999; Iggers, 1998; Rosen, 1999). The varieties of public journalism share an emphasis on civic engagement and embrace of the public interest (Iggers, 1998; Romano, 2010). Another important strand of many arguments against, or at least scepticism about, the prospects of professional journalism, especially given the possibilities the internet now offers, is that they represent a critique of for-profit corporate news media. Often, anti-professionalism stands in for, or implies, an anti-capitalist press position. The concomitant argument holds that questions of news access, diversity and inclusiveness – that is to say, versions of media democracy – will never be resolved without a decentralization of media resources, that mitigates the influence of powerful, commercial media organizations.

If we can discern a general reaction to the optimistic position on new technology and journalism, such a counter-position can be characterized as a fierce defence of the profession of journalism, leavened with scepticism and pessimism about the prospects of the new internet-enabled platform for media to change indispensable aspects of what journalism is. Again, there is a wide range of opinions and arguments in this corner but I'll endeavour to identify some common elements.

The key counter-argument of those arguing that new technology does not fundamentally change the profession is as follows: journalism as a profession, especially as tied to newspapers, has developed core skills and social functions that cannot be substantially replaced by participatory journalism models centring on the internet:

> Newspaper workers are the canaries in the coal mine of journalism, and by extension of the modern public sphere … . [N]ewspapers, because of their larger staffs, continue to do the heavy lifting of original newsgathering, investigative and critical reporting. It is because of this fact that spreading layoffs and labour rationalization at newspapers is critical: for what is at risk arguably goes well beyond a failed business model.
>
> (Compton, 2010, p. 599)

These skills and dispositions represented by journalism and the value placed upon them vary but typically include: reporting; investigatory skills; research; critical analysis; fact-checking; objectivity; commitment to truth; quality of analysis and writing (Media Entertainment and Arts Alliance, 2008). Typically this defence concentrates on making a case in support of quality journalism. However, nuanced versions of the defence of journalism, as it formerly exists, also raise questions about how important but specialized kinds of reporting and coverage survive – such as court reporting or financial journalism. These kinds of journalism not only attach to, and have a close relationship with, particular kinds of institutions – such as courts or bourses – through which they gain privileged access to information and news, but they also require expertise and knowledge built up over a long period of time (Örnebring, 2010; Schudson, 2008).

So far I have identified two broad currents in thinking about the future of journalism as a profession, while freely admitting this is very much a generalization. Fortunately there are alternatives to the bifurcation of debate between overblown optimism regarding new technology, on the one hand, versus essentially unreconstructed defences of the importance of traditional journalism. In particular, there are a growing number of commentators and scholars who urge the adoption of a critical perspective on technology, but contend that the implications of the growing reliance on transformed digital-media platforms are far more complex than previously thought, much more optimistic and disturbing, but in ways not commonly understood. A key scholar of media and new technologies who believes that there is nothing to be gained in crying tears over the spilt milk of traditional journalism is Mark Deuze. Deuze's research has focused upon understanding the changing nature of media work. His book *Media Work* (Deuze, 2007) looks in particular at the heightened, pervasive role of creativity in the precarious kind of labour that characterizes much contemporary work in the media. Deuze also considers the distinction, or yawning gulf, between journalists and journalism – that is, a restricted notion of the profession of journalism, and the much more expansive, dynamic practices that make up journalism. In a paper co-authored paper with Italian technology scholar Leopoldina Fortunati, he suggests:

> we see a situation evolving in the field of journalism where power is increasingly flowing in two directions: that of the owners, shareholders, business partners, editors and publishers of news organisations, and that of TPFKATA [the people formerly known as the audience]. In both instances, the power – to tell stories, to earn a living, to enjoy professional freedom and protections – is being sapped away from

the people democratic societies used to rely on for their news and information: journalists.

(Deuze and Fortunati, 2010, p. 165)

Deuze and Fortunati argue that:

> The shift of power from journalists towards publishers might be characterised by two stages: the first has seen journalism's domestication by publishers (and editors) ... as exemplified by journalism's overreliance on the ruling elite and its spokespeople for setting the agenda and serving as sources for news. The second stage has seen the publishers de-structuring journalism by using the Internet and deploying the utopian concept of the networked organisation – redesigning the profession as simple, immaterial labour ... .
>
> (Deuze and Fortunati, 2010, p. 166)

In order to make sense of the changes in journalism as a profession, Deuze and Fortunati contend that we must pay attention not only to the changes in the audience, and new alliances being made with journalists (not least because of the worsening situation of employment), but also we must reckon with the general shift of power to the employer:

> what Rosen and others tend to neglect or underestimate is another equally if not more powerful redistribution of power taking place in the contemporary media ecosystem: a sapping of economic and cultural power away from professional journalists to what can be called 'the people formerly known as the employers.'
>
> (Deuze and Fortunati, 2010)

They suggest it is important to view journalists as part of the category of 'immaterial labour workers', part of the:

> huge, horizontal working-class sector submitted to what [Richard] Sennett (2006) has called the culture of the 'new' capitalism. In this restructuring of labour relations, workers are expected to continuously adapt, 'self-program', to flexible production processes and new technological demands – all without the support and investment of their employers, of course.
>
> (Deuze and Fortunati, 2010, p. 172)

In making this argument, Deuze and Fortunati draw upon a body of Italian theory about types of 'abstract' or 'immaterial' work and labour (Brophy and de Peuter, 2007; De Angelis, 2007; Lazzarato, 1996, 1997; Negri, 2008), as well as cultural sociologist Richard Sennett's work on capitalism, its restructuring of work and its implications for people's lives and identities (Sennett, 1998, 2006, 2008). What they are suggesting is that work under contemporary capitalist societies has fundamentally changed in nature. Thus it is crucial to understand the changes in journalism as a profession in this light. The relations of the economy and work provide crucial contexts for understanding what is happening with new technology and media.

Another important figure who manages to steer between the Scylla of new technology and Charybdis of stout journalism is the eminent American sociologist Michael Schudson, who has offered an important critique of traditional journalism. With the advent of technology-fuelled visions of journalism and its tipping point, Schudson has undertaken some detailed studies of new journalism and old journalism, and provides a careful diagnosis of problems and prospects. Evaluating the new media during the 2008 US presidential elections, Schudson reflects:

> What holds the American nation together? In the 1790s, the answer to that question in the minds of many national politicians was, 'very, very little'. They did not have great confidence that the union would endure … . How is this different today?
>
> (Schudson, 2009, pp. 16–17)

Schudson's preliminary conclusion is that

> the new media have provided a source for an anarchistic, populist element to insert itself visibly and vocally into political campaigns as a disorganising force playing off against the most ambitious, organised efforts at mass mobilisation, apart from war, that Americans ever engage in.
>
> (Schudson, 2009, p. 17)

He elaborates further:

> It may be that the technological changes all around us and the cultural changes, too – *The Daily Show* and *The Colbert Report* are products not of a new technology but of a newly exploitable cultural

opening for irreverence – will become familiar, will settle into predictable patterns. Perhaps traditional centres of economic and political power that seemed shaken in 2008 will regain control, but that does not seem likely in the near future. The new media singly and collectively are sponsors of a new intensity, ubiquity, and anarchism in our mediated public world.

(Schudson, 2009, p. 19)

Schudson's comments were published before the US mid-term election in late 2010, which saw the ultra-conservative and hyper-populist Tea Party become the beneficiaries of a strong turn against Barack Obama's Democrats. This was a plebiscite in which the use of new technologies by progressives was not the celebrated motif (as in the election of Barack Obama in 2008). Rather the stand-out for liberals was Stephen Colbert and Jon Stewart's 'Rally to Restore Sanity and/or Fear', a parody event attended by an estimated 250,000 New Yorkers (Molloy and Boyle, 2010).

Schudson is but one of a number of analysts who argue for, and enact, a careful analysis of the role and shaping of new technology in journalism. Via a revisionist appropriation of the important US intellectual Walter Lippman, Schudson argues that what we take to be the extraordinary effects of our contemporary news and media ecology are not, in fact, the sole consequence of new technologies. Drawing on emerging histories of the internet, Schudson points to the influence of social, cultural and political movements in how the medium is imagined (Schudson, 2010, pp. 4–5). Schudson proposes that this ecology of news is dependent as much as anything else on what he, after Walter Lippman, terms 'political observatories' – agencies and sources of public information outside of journalism, producing reports, analysis and independent advice. According to Schudson, these 'political observatories', desired by Lippman, started to effectively materialize in the 1970s with the rise of non-profit research and advocacy organizations (for instance, in the area of human rights), but also with the reform legislation of the 1970s and 1980s that saw government monitoring itself and also private corporations through relatively independent agencies and making reports and other information available (Schudson, 2010, p. 5). Taking up new media theorist Lev Manovich's remark about the centrality of the database to the digital age, Schudson argues that while a 'database is not journalism ... increasingly, sophisticated journalism depends on quality downloadable, searchable databases' (Schudson, 2010, p. 8). Schudson contends that:

Political observatories do not replace journalists, nor do databases shove narratives aside. But the observatories are increasingly valuable partners for journalists, and databases lay new foundations for narrative. Both offer promise for developing the kind of public information that makes democracy possible.

(Schudson, 2010, pp. 8–9)

What Schudson's analysis points to is the large settings of technology in which new trends in the media are embedded, which in fact belong to much longer historical and political trajectories. He is but one of a growing number of scholars seeking to engage critically and imaginatively yet realistically with the politics and characteristics of the new technologies. As heated debate rages on the future of journalism as a profession, such critical perspectives are especially helpful as we move into the closely related issue of media institutions, their characteristics, continuities, politics and transformations.

Media Institutions Old and New

As one moves through debates on new technology and media professions, one inevitably comes up against questions of what is to be valued and supported in the work and vocation of media. Institutions are a key concern in media, but are often overlooked. This may be because institutions often take a conservative stance and function in media – something that is especially counter-intuitive or opposed to the helter-skelter, destructive, capitalist forces of new technology.

I am not the first to suggest that institutions have an indispensable role to play in the unfolding of new technologies and the media. In the brief space available, I want to explore this through discussion of two kinds of institutions. First, public-service (or -sector) broadcasting is a widespread phenomenon across many countries, with various forms, and is undergoing intense change. Previously thought to be superseded or moribund, public-service organizations are now talked about as 'public-service media', and are widely viewed as engines of new media innovation. Second, new institutions have been designed to address the coming crisis of the press. With the commercial press widely believed to be going to hell in a handcart – or at least search engine, courtesy of Google, Baidu and fraternal technologies – there is a renewed, widespread interest in creating new institutions – through public funding or dedicated foundations – to support quality journalism. Taken together, the two institutions – one old, and one new – are now being discussed as part of an overarching response to the dilemmas, opportunities and characteristics of new media.

The Rise and Rise of Public-Service Media

In the 1990s, public-sector broadcasting was widely believed to be in crisis, and indeed some critics considered its future to be very bleak indeed. Author of the definitive jeremiad *The Decline and Fall of Public Sector Broadcasting* (Tracey, 1998), Michael Tracey colourfully opined:

> Public broadcasting is a bit like the Weimar Republic in the late 1920s, it's a corpse on leave. I don't think it has a future, to be honest, and I think that is not good news for all of us, but I do not think it has a serious future.
>
> (Tracey, quoted in O'Regan, 2000)

During the 1980s and into the 1990s, market-based policies had progressively deepened their hold and broadened their reach. While the commercialization of media gathered pace and its rationales became elaborated and achieved an orthodoxy, the state withdrew from provision of goods and service in many areas, including media. This had immediate effects in Europe where public broadcasting had been the dominant form in television in particular. In pursuit of a common market for the European Communities the 1989 EC directive *Television without Frontiers* sought to ensure 'the transition from national markets to a common programme production and distribution market and to establish conditions of fair competition without prejudice to the public interest role to be discharged by the television broadcasting services' (Council of the European Communities, 1989). As the language of the directive illustrates, the new emphasis on reaching beyond national television and markets to pan-European markets was not a neutral move. It brought into tension ideas of 'competition' (and what was 'fair') and the 'public interest'. With the many changes that occurred in television over this period, combining with the greater range and type of programming and changes to formats and content that commercialization and diversification of broadcasting platforms and licences especially brought about, state funding of broadcasting struggled to maintain its traditional rationales and find new ones.

A key issue raised by market-based policies was why should governments fund media at all – if commercial organizations could do so more-or-less satisfactorily? The conventional answer by proponents of market-based policies (which we have earlier talked about as neoclassical economics or neoliberalism) is that the government should only fund goods and services deemed as necessary for citizens, but which markets have failed to provide. In the area of television and radio, the special contribution of the institutions of public-sector broadcasters was typically thought to reside in elements such as: quality programming; special-interest programmes; programmes for minority audiences (such as cultural and linguistic minorities); vital news and current affairs; children's programmes; and content of national significance (relating to national traditions or cultural heritages). With the retreat of the expansive welfare state, governments retreated from many domains, privatizing postal services, telecommunications and even broadcasting. With the rise of the 'new management', or 'corporate managerialism', policies, values and financial frameworks formerly associated with businesses were applied to government organizations (or 'enterprises'). The consequence for public broadcasters was a constant tightening of budgets. This was helpful for governments in many cases, because it helped keep public broadcasters on a tight leash – reminding them in forceful ways that editorial independence would come at a cost.

At first the new technologies represented by the internet, new telecommunications and digital television promised to add fuel to the bonfire of the public broadcasters' vanities and rationales. Here were even more media channels, programmes and content, and possibilities for communication. Why, in a sea of plenty, were government-funded public broadcasters needed – when new entrants enabled by the greater scope of new media, as well as citizens doing-it-themselves, could provide the materials and resources and channels needed for the national conversation? And why, in a multichannel world of many audiences and publics, did we still believe that public broadcasters could claim a national purpose of serving all citizens – when they had actually often been woeful at recognizing different needs, tending to focus on upper- and middle-class cultural elites?

As the internet developed, a curious thing happened. In a number of countries, public-sector broadcasters figured prominently in the vanguard of cultural innovation centring on the new technology. In Australia, for instance, staff from various strands of programming at the national broadcaster ABC experimented with the internet, often having recourse to external providers and practical work-arounds to find ways of using online technology (Burns, 2008; Martin, 2004). Such pioneering work long preceded official ABC policies to extend its remit to the internet. By the early 2000s, however, the ABC website was something of a national treasure – one of the most visited websites in the country, and a trove of innovative online broadcasting efforts. Later it was the ABC that pioneered podcasting in Australia. In Britain, the BBC, which had the advantage of a solid revenue base from licence fees (rather than annual appropriations from the government), became a world leader in reinventing public-service broadcasting in a digital age.

As media convergence developed through the 2000s, there was greater recognition of the value of the brand alongside the 'backlist' or archive of respected, desired content. Corporations vied with each other to acquire copyright to backlists of music and rights to old movies. Institutions, such as the BBC, held collections of programmes, of great value, depth and breadth. Such content could be sold or licensed to raise revenue or make a profit. Alternatively, given that the content had been produced with taxpayer money, as the phrase goes, it could be made publicly available as a collection. Prior to the internet, there was no easy or cheap way to broadcast or make available this wealth of content. Now there was – as the BBC demonstrated with its moves to make its archive of material publicly available. Ironically, it turned out that with the rise of digital-media technology, public-service broadcasters were needed more than ever. While many tensions remain about what the public interest(s) in broadcasting might be, critics such as Peter Golding and Graham Murdock can feel vindicated, in warning that

> in the digital era, the BBC will need more than ever to be the flag carrier for a public service committed to providing for full citizenship and social inclusion rather than consumption and individual life style.
>
> (Golding and Murdock, 2001)

When the BBC had its Royal Charter of Incorporation renewed in 2006 (indeed printed on vellum, sealed and laid in Parliament), this was explicitly recognized as a reason why it should have a continued existence. Thus the Charter's preamble states Her Majesty's opinion that:

> in view of the widespread interest which is taken by Our People in services which provide audio and visual material by means of broadcasting or the use of newer technologies, and of the great value of such services as means of disseminating information, education and entertainment, We believe it to be in the interests of Our People that

there should continue to be an independent corporation and that it should provide such services ... .

(Department for Culture, Media and Sport, 2006)

In its response to the government's Charter review, the BBC had enunciated a view of itself as playing a leading role in the national imperative of creating a 'digital' Britain, by 'building public value' (Terrington and Dollar, 2005): 'Creating a fully digital Britain is a public challenge which the BBC must help to lead. It is a Britain from which the BBC, and only the BBC, can ensure that no one is excluded' (BBC, 2005).

Inflecting various givens of the policy climate, the BBC acknowledged the need to be as efficient and 'small' as possible in line with the reigning economic imperatives, but bold too:

> An economist might conclude from this that the BBC has an important role in preventing various kinds of market failure in the new digital world. Yes – but our vision is far bolder than that suggests. We look forward to a future where the public have access to a treasure-house of digital content, a store of value which spans media and platforms, develops and grows over time, which the public own and can freely use in perpetuity. A future where the historic one-way traffic of content from broadcaster to consumer evolves into a true creative dialogue in which the public are not passive audiences but active, inspired participants.

(BBC, 2005)

This role for the BBC was endorsed in the Charter, with its galvanizing role in new technologies added to its public purposes:

(a) sustaining citizenship and civil society;
(b) promoting education and learning;
(c) stimulating creativity and cultural excellence;
(d) representing the UK, its nations, regions and communities;
(e) bringing the UK to the world and the world to the UK;
(f) in promoting its other purposes, *helping to deliver to the public the benefit of emerging communications technologies and services and, in addition, taking a leading role in the switchover to digital television.*
    (Department for Culture Media and Sport, 2006; my emphasis)

These public purposes are spelt out in its framework agreement with the government, including details of how the Charter will be implemented.

Here the digital switchover merits its own section, but otherwise new technology is largely seen as implicit to achieving the BBC's mandate (Department for Culture Media and Sport, 2006).

The BBC is but one public-service media organization (Tambini and Cowling, 2004). However, the BBC had long been an important international broadcaster, listened to and watched in many countries. Its digital ventures represent a much-discussed and debated instance of how publicly funded media organizations can and should respond to the manifold challenges of the present age – especially those issues associated with new technology. The BBC's historical legacy and contemporary digital response has certainly been influential not only in Anglophone countries and those of its former Commonwealth but elsewhere also. That said, there are many other international responses to new technology from public-service media organizations whose pathways, options and cultures are fashioned in very different ways, that I will not be able to discuss here (Barsamian, 2002; Gardam and Levy, 2008; Petros and Iosifidis, 2007; Raboy, 1995; Vissol, 2006). Instead, for the purpose of succinctly outlining key challenges for media institutions, I wish to stay with the public-service media theme, and look at the call for the creation of new institutions beyond both existing public-service media organizations and commercial media – to underpin desired kinds of journalism and news.

The New Public Trust in the Press

With the established economic basis for the press seriously under challenge, how is it possible to sustain the institutions of which commercial newspapers and magazines have been the custodians (deliberately or unwittingly). The financial pressures facing media organizations have led to job losses in journalism for some time. Newsrooms and press bureaux are not as well funded or widespread as they previously were. Editors of a comparative book on the business of journalism urge caution, arguing that the US 'may well be more of an exception and less of a forerunner than is sometimes assumed in discussions of international media developments' (Nielsen and Levy, 2010a, p. 13). Nielsen and Levy believe that 'it is premature to announce the death of the newspaper, of television, and certainly of commercial news organizations more widely' (Nielsen and Levy, 2010a, p. 13). They can find no evidence for the proposition that the 'business of journalism has reached the end of the line, that the current crisis is terminal for the industry or the vocation it has sustained' (Nielsen and Levy, 2010b, pp. 143–4). Rather, they suggest that:

All around the world ... new generations of managers and journalists are reinventing the business and the profession, and charitable foundations and governments are considering what role *they* can play in making sure professional journalism underwritten by privately profitable commercial news media can continue to play a publicly valuable role in our democracies.

(Nielsen and Levy, 2010b, p. 144)

Others take a different view. In any case, as we have seen, there is widespread debate about the identification of the valorized traditions of journalism with the commercial media.

If newspapers do continue to close in many countries, or at least significantly modify their operations to employ fewer journalists, then a well-accepted, reasonably stable source of training, identity and support for the professional exercise of journalism is being seriously diminished. There is an argument that although traditional jobs in journalism are being cut and not replaced, new positions and kinds of career paths are opening up, not only in new forms of media (online; mobile) but also in other occupations where the skills and experience of journalists are increasingly welcomed and relied upon (public and media relations; organization and political communications). Granted such a displacement and substitution of journalistic work, it remains unclear – and indeed is a subject of intense contention – how and whether this shift will reconstitute sufficient institutional support for the various roles of journalism its consumers, publics and stakeholders desire. What is clear is that there is a pressing need to understand the new balance required among different kinds of media, especially between private, commercial interests and publicly supported organizations. Nielsen and Levy usefully summarize the key elements of such an inquiry:

(a) what sustainable balance can be found between the elements of journalism that are public goods and the rest of journalism;

(b) how one can ensure the provision of those elements that truly are important for democracies and that the market alone is unlikely to deliver;

(c) what mix of market, civil society, and public provision is then desirable and;

(d) how the result can be made available – across any number of platforms – to the wider population who is supposed to benefit from it all, and in terms of whose interest intervention can be legitimised in the first place. (Nielsen and Levy, 2010b, pp. 145–6)

Earlier in this chapter, we have seen a renewed set of public rationales for public-service media to deliver aspects of media felt to be necessary to a polity, but not satisfactorily provided by the massive commercial and corporate media sector. New ideas have also emerged about the funding of journalism.

As we have noted, for some decades there has been an acceptance in many countries of the need to provide public support, very often through direct government funding, or licensed and regulated schemes, to broadcasters. The public has grown accustomed to the notion that there were public-sector or -service, or just plain public (as in the US) organizations broadcasting radio and television, and in doing so, they were providing characteristic types of information and entertainment. There was little support for the suggestion that the public purse should fund newspapers. In the twentieth century, government funding of newspapers was commonly associated with what used to be termed the 'second world' – that is, the countries of the Soviet bloc and Communist world such as China. Famous press titles such as the Soviet Communist *Pravda* ('Truth'), the Chinese *People's Daily* and, still surviving in its original role as party mouth-piece, the Cuban official newspaper *Granma*. In the first world and third world, there may also have been newspapers funded and controlled by particular political or commercial groupings, such as political parties, but there was much suspicion about governments funding the press. Such arrangements were felt to compromise the role of the press as the 'Fourth Estate', independent and able to be critical of government.

Surprisingly, the question of government funding for newspapers has been recently canvassed in the West, in two main ways.

First, new trusts and foundations have emerged to provide support for particular types of journalism – especially public-interest, investigative and quality journalism. Such institutions have already played a significant role in journalism. In the field of civic and public journalism (Ettema and Glasser, 1998), several charitable trusts and independent non-profit organizations – notably the Pew Charitable Trusts (with its Pew Centre for Civic Journalism) founded projects in the 1990s especially (Loomis and Meyer, 2000; Woo, 2000). A renewed emphasis is being placed on the role of non-profit organizations in the provision of news. A 2005 manifesto formulated by a group of journalists and scholars in a gathering at the University of Pennsylvania made this its first point: 'greater role for nonprofits – organizations such as the Center for Public Integrity, the *St Petersburg Times* and National Public Radio, along with foundation support – could help lift all media' (Overholser, 2006,

p. 3). Philip Meyer points out that charitable foundations have moved in to 'fill gaps left by short-sighted application of the profit motive', such as the training of journalists, but also 'direct efforts to pay for news' (Meyer, 2009, p. 224). Whereas advertisers have previously been the clear and present danger to journalistic independence, foundations themselves have their own interests (Poynter Institute, 2001). Meyer acknowledges the issues, but believes it is on balance no worse than substantially advertiser-funded newspapers: 'Allowing charitable foundations to pay for the news might be risky, but it is probably no worse than a system in which advertisers pay for it' (Meyer, 2004, p. 226). Since then, the potential role of non-profit organizations has broadened. On the table now are proposals that go well beyond the notion of supplementing news by commissioning content to the fully fledged business of underwriting whole media organizations. This was envisaged in the 2005 manifesto, with a suggestion that there was a need for new non-profit media models, which should be predicated on policy changes from the government including 'tax legislation to enable news companies to be organized as nonprofit, tax-exempt corporations' and a 'government-sponsored search engine' (Overholser, 2006, p. 21).

Second, the most obvious model for obtaining a non-profit vehicle for maintaining newspapers has been the notion of a trust. Perhaps the best example of an existing well-respected newspaper funded through a trust is the *Guardian*. Established in 1821, ownership of the paper passed in 1907 from its founder's son, John Edward Taylor, to C. P. Scott, who edited it for fifty-seven years, and eventually to his surviving son John Russell Scott, who soon gave it to the Scott Trust – thereafter responsible for its radical editorial tradition and securing the *Guardian*'s finances (*Guardian*, 2008). Trusts are now being used not only to secure newspapers, but also to ensure a stable financial basis for their new media equivalents. Hybrid forms of online newspapers emerged early on as email lists or websites often underpinned by subscription (*Craigslist* being the oft-quoted example). With so many websites and blogs available, sustaining good journalism became an issue for many, especially as subscription – which had worked for many specialist papers, magazines and journals – failed to provide sufficient backing. Other institutions have also stepped into the breach to provide resources, infrastructure, profile and other kinds of support for news ventures. Universities have long offered support for independent journalism and news ventures, and are now supporting or publishing blogs.

Trusts can offer a way to ensure an economic and organizational platform to support journalism as a profession – hence the interest they are currently attracting. However, there are other ways to use the general idea of trusts to strengthen the role of journalism. This can be seen in the idea of 'trust principles', a way to safeguard the separation between a media company and its editorial and journalism operations. The leading news agency Reuters, which merged with information giant Thomson in 2008, devised 'trust principles' in 1941, that imposed 'obligations on Reuters and its employees to act at all times with integrity, independence and freedom from bias' (Thomson Reuters, 2011). The directors of the Thomson Reuters board are obliged to have due regard to the principles, and a further safeguard is provided by the Thomson Reuters Founders Share Company. The Founders Share Company was a mechanism created in 1984 when Reuters become a public company, and its directors are especially charged with ensuring that the trust principles are complied with – providing feedback to the board.

Conclusion

As discussed in this chapter, an important debate is in progress about journalism as a profession. Many journalists are deeply pessimistic about what the future holds – and whether there will be sufficient jobs, at appropriate pay, at all levels of the press. Moves to outsource key jobs, such as copy-editing, are viewed with dismay and suspicion. Most journalists now make do with fewer resources and support for their work than they did in the past. However, others hold divergent views. As we have seen, some journalists and many outside the profession hold an optimistic view about the future. The basis for such optimism varies, from those who believe that new technologies and their related developments offer the potential to greatly open up and improve journalism through a kind of bracing anti-professionalism, to those who point to the continued growth of journalism as a whole, even if it is across the kind of popular media outlets and organizations that have been of lower status in the profession and less valued socially (McNair, 2009). In the discussions on new technology and media professions, political economy is paramount. This is because new technology takes shape amid the shifting patterns of ownership, control, structure, forms and power relations of newspapers. So framed, new technology lies at the heart of debates about whether the business model can sustain newspapers, as advertising migrates elsewhere. Newspapers continue to be a vitally important form of journalism because of their nexus to democracy and the political process. Moreover, the profession as a consequence is under threat at the same time as new media competition exacerbates more long-standing challenges to notions of professionalism.

The conversation about the future of journalism has close ties to debates about the institutions of the media, especially the public ones. In addition to the prominence of trusts and foundations as institutions for supporting journalism, the broader role of government as a key supporter of public media in many countries is being considered. This widening discussion is a consequence of the way that debates unfolded regarding public-service broadcasting. I have noted the shift from talk of public-sector 'broadcasting' to public 'media', 'communication' and 'information' (Vissol, 2006). In some ways, these vocabularies enlarge the sphere of what was clearly and narrowly defined as types of broadcasting to engage a much wider, pervasive sphere of media and communication. Yet other shifts in concepts and terms dismantle – or, as theorists of competition would say 'unbundle' – public media.

According to some, for instance, what public broadcasters no longer do is provide a cohesive, coherent and indivisible set of services, bound together with a worldview and philosophy. Rather like all other contemporary media companies, they provide 'content'. If content is king of this policy paradigm, then it could feasibly be provided by a range of other more fluid institutions or policy, service and purchasing arrangements. This is potentially very good for increasing competition in content paid for by public funds, as happens already with public broadcasters commissioning television and film programming from independent production houses), thus adding to 'plurality' of supply and diversity of public-media content (Elstein, 2008). The implication of such a focus on content, combined with changed needs for citizens in the new media landscape, may mean that the role of the public-service broadcaster becomes akin to an authoritative super-filter – the BBC meets Google:

> In the digital world, the most important role of the PSB [public-sector broadcaster] may therefore be as a validator and editor, the trusted filter that authenticates the value of whatever content it offers ... . The digital world is incorrigibly plural ... . [The] PSB in the digital age can still be the sextant by which the consumer and citizen can navigate the content on which an informed democracy and culturally self-aware society is built.
>
> (Gardam, 2008, p. 21)

Whether one subscribes to the reinvention of public institutions as 'filters', rather than arbiters of taste, or guardians of national cultural heritage, there is now much up for grabs. Richard Collins has suggested that we do need to take seriously the question of which media institutions should be funded by governments. Collins has noted that the BBC, while still restricted in its funding, still receives a substantial sum of money. Whereas if support for the media is needed, in light of the market failure and other shortcomings of trends inextricably linked to the new technologies, in order to sustain and rekindle quality journalism and news, then perhaps it is time to rethink traditional assumptions about the central role of one, or a small set, of national broadcasting institutions – as opposed to a 'public-service publisher' that could 'diversify, pluralise and incentivise innovation in a rather ossified public-service broadcasting regime' (Collins, 2010). This is a scary proposition for many of us who see public-service media as a vital part of the old and new media. Yet, it is surely a proposition that is heading in the right direction of rethinking institutions, and professions, to genuinely respond to the challenges of new technologies.

6 New Media Concerns

Much in media today has to do with new technologies. Many varied technologies are involved in the media – in all aspects of production, distribution and consumption. We are no longer simply concerned with 'big' media: feature-length movies best viewed on cinema screens; television programmes watched by the majority of a nation's citizens, that cost substantial sums of money to make; radio programmes that require producers, researchers, technicians and managers; newspapers that involve highly trained journalists, seasoned editors, vast and expensive printing presses, lucrative advertising sections and extensive networks of newsagents, newspaper stands, paperboys and papergirls, or home-delivery agents. *The* media also encompasses 'little' media: Facebook friends; Twitterers and Tweets; mash-ups made and watched on laptops; portable and personal media from Nintendo DS and Sony PlayStation and portable music players through cameras and wised-up mobile phones to iPads; domestic WiFi and home media centres; GPS and satnav devices; internet-connected cars and fridges; and little chips in lots of things connected to all sorts of networks. In the face of the immensity of all this – these technologies, their relationships with other machines, with people, with non-human objects and actors, with the environment, and how all of this impinges on our ultimate topic of the media – this book has mainly focused upon digital networks, especially those involved with the internet and mobile media. Even in this realm of new technology, you'd have to say that there is a fair bit going on.

The size and scale of online and mobile media continue to grow. In 1999, people thought of the internet as an avenue to things like email, the web, chat rooms, instant messaging and games – while markets were excited about its potential to create the new economy. By 2005, these ideas about the internet had radically changed, and the prominent elements of the technology included broadband, blogs, peer-to-peer networks, voice-over internet protocol communications, podcasting, WiFi, lots of games, plus the earlier applications. The internet had metastatized again by 2011, spawning social media, apps, mobile internet, video over internet protocol communication, internet television, as well as what had gone before. A sign of the times was the announcement that Facebook CEO and founder, Mark Zuckerberg had been proclaimed *Time* magazine person of the year for 2010, as the total number of Facebook users soared over the 500 million mark. Since then, internet and mobile-based social media have proliferated markedly in their types, reach and domination of internet, and are widely believed by media companies, advertisers, marketers, government and many ordinary people to be fundamentally reshaping the way media work.

If the internet and mobile media expand rapidly and change shape every few years, their influence on other media only appears to be expanding and taking new forms too. What we have understood and valued as the press – high, middle- and low-brow, broadsheet and tabloid, mainstream, trade and specialist newspapers – is in ferment. In particular, internet-related and enhanced phenomena – such as rich and quickly available sources of information, online news, low-cost, high-impact publishing and distribution possibilities, Search, open-source news, Twitter, dismantling and re-aggregation of global audiences, media possibilities for historically neglected publics and communities – are interacting in complex, multifaceted ways with other dynamics in the press. Like everyone else, television and radio broadcasters are puzzled about the fragmentation, dispersal and incurable multitasking of audiences – scratching their heads about how they can possibly reach the breadth of audiences via programmes and material tailored to particular platforms, and how they can possibly reconfigure their media organizations to respond to both old and new media habits and cultures.

Truly there is great deal unfolding in the media that pivots upon new technologies. Yet, as I have argued in this book, there is a core of myths, misconceptions and misunderstandings of technology that we need to confront, before we can really get to the heart of the matter. In Chapter 2, I argued that much discussion of new technologies mystifies and obscures the dynamics at play. A strong, critical understanding of new technologies, therefore, is critical to understanding what the new kinds of media genres, practices and cultures are, and what their implications are for audiences, professions and institutions. For students of media, this means carefully assessing the precise nature and characteristics of technologies and discerning the ways and contexts in which they unfold. In this concluding chapter, then, I want to draw together two sets of issues and arguments that percolate through this book and are key to understanding new technologies and the media: how to study technology; and how to understand and engage with the new concerns that the present phase of technology-centred media raises.

On Not Taking Technology for Granted

Technology figures heavily in all our lives, whether we love, loathe or are indifferent to it. As students of the media, we have a tremendous opportunity not only to gain an understanding of the role of new technologies in this immediate area, but also to arrive at a new appreciation that will be of assistance in other areas of everyday life. The fundamental approach that I have outlined here is a critical one. As it appears in the media, and in other domains, much about technology is very often taken for granted. This might seem an odd contention, given that the novelty of technology is typically believed to reside in its power to disrupt the status quo, and to radically rework what has gone before its arrival. The still dominant view, as I have explained, is, at base, tantamount to technology determinism. While all too common, technology determinism does not help us to analyze what such technology is, what accompanies it and what occurs as a result, and what its implications might be.

A critical approach to technology can be informed by many different theories, to some of which I have alluded. Whatever perspective taken, the critical approach is helpful because its starting point and basic orientation is to observe, document, analyze, interpret and construct an account of what technology is, how it operates, what discourses and meanings are associated with it, and who and what support it. In short, how technology is put together. After all, technology is not something that falls from the heavens, or rolls off the production lines of corporations, after ingenious inventors and designers conjure it up. Technology is an achievement, in all senses of the word. Its immense power, solidity, pervasive effects on and incorporation into our lives is made possible by a mix of many factors. In the making of new technology, we find that new cultural forms, new kinds of social relations, and new ideas about society are all involved. The critical disposition and training that students of media have long been urged to devote to studying texts and programmes, learning about industry structures and government policies, coming to grips with audiences, uses and practices, also need to be extended to the analysis and interpretation of technology.

Forearmed with a critical approach, the engagement with new technologies and the media can proceed. The first challenge always lies in the comprehension of technical characteristics. It is important to gain a clear sense of what is possible at any point in time with technologies – and what is not. In Chapter 2, for instance, I provide an overview of key aspects of digital networks. This treatment is very much aimed at the layperson. It is useful to know, however, that it is always possible – and often necessary – to delve deeper into an area of new technology, by seeking the appropriate level of technical knowledge, explanation and advice. For those of us, like me, unencumbered by a formal training in science and technology, there are many primers on new technologies aimed at different audiences. Regulators, policy agencies and governments are excellent sources of plain-language guides to new technologies, because they are often required to produce overviews and reports for policy makers, elected representatives and interested citizens.

After gaining a basic technical understanding, the media student needs to attend to the task of observation and documentation. Key questions that can orient study and discussion here can be generated and addressed by attending carefully to the processes in which the technology is shaped and takes form. Different angles and focii are possible here:

Histories: How did the technology appear? Who and what was involved in its invention and development? What did people imagine would be its main uses and significance? How was it actually adopted, resisted or ignored? Was the technology used differently by different groups of people, or in different parts of the world?

Ideas and Emotions: What are the ideas or discourses associated with particular new technologies? Who are thought to be early adopters of the technology? What do people think they do with the technology? What are the affects and emotions associated with the technology?

Media: How does the technology fit into or disrupt existing media? Are there new companies and organizations responsible for delivering new kinds of media associated with the technology? How should we characterize these? What are the economic co-ordinates and business models underpinning the technology? Who are the audiences and publics that come into being – or realign – with the technology? How do our ideas about what media is (and what it does) change along with this technology?

Culture and the Social: How do people use the technology now? What do users do with it, and with whom do they do it? How is it configured, designed and arranged? What is its 'communicative architecture'? What is the particular culture associated with it? How does the technology relate to the larger culture? How are relations among different groups of people, and groups of things, altered, or believed to be altered, through the introduction of the technology?

There are many challenges associated with studying new technology, especially when evaluating the significance of a new technology for the media.

Consider the sheer volume of new technologies, that grace the market each year and the millennial claims that usually accompany them. We might call 2010 the Facebook moment, complete with its own film of the *Zeitgeist*, *The Social Network* (Fincher, 2010). Yet how do we know whether – or perhaps when – the looming global domination of Facebook will crumble and it become just another social network – à la Orkut, MySpace or Friendsters – or even just another mundane part of the internet. This happened to earlier technologies, such as MUDS and MOOs, webcams and hundreds of wannabe software programs and internet technologies. Many of these still have their followers but no longer command the allegiance or warrant the great expectations of markets or users. Each technology has its own obvious period of first flush of enthusiasm and fervid embrace by users dazzled by the new capabilities, before things settle down, or take another turn. Theorists of technology diffusion famously categorize such patterns. However, the careers of technology, as their biographies reveal, can take all manner of unexpected twists and turns, that defy the capabilities of investors, retailers, futurists and punters alike, to predict where, in the crowded pantheons of media, a given technology might come to rest at any given point.

The unpredictable nature of new technologies is simply an occupational hazard for the media student committed to their serious contemplation. Looked at over a five-year period, Facebook could be huge. Considered over a decade, let alone the span of fifty, 100 or 1,000 years, Facebook, the concept of social-networking systems or even the rage for social media, could turn out to be a relatively transitory thing, perhaps the mere curiosity of a period, or whimsy of a particular society, group or subculture. Yet the careful study of a technology and its imbrication in a formation of media is a worthwhile thing in its own right. A critical investigation of technology can provide real insights into what media are and how they work. It can also reveal profound things about the very nature of technology, and how it allows us to connect with others (the social), as well as making a fundamental contribution to our customs, practices, ideas and meanings, and way of life (culture).

Old Stories, New Questions

As we have seen, new technologies bring with them with new possibilities and openings for the media. In Chapter 3, we explored the rise of online and mobile news, and how distinct kinds of news gathering and reporting, dissemination and consumption are associated with these. The impact of such changes upon the press is far from certain. Websites of major media outlets have gained acceptance, after fifteen years or so of experimentation. So too have new internet-based outlets, including the *Drudge Report, Huffington Post*, OhmyNews and Salon.com. Blogs are relatively well established and serve various functions across the news, current affairs, information and entertainment continuum the press spans. Many users, especially those who are young, affluent and in particular social and cultural groupings, get the news more frequently via Twitter, favourite blogs, apps and social-networking systems, through new kinds of personal as much as public filters, than through mainstream media. Thus the interweaving of new and old media continues apace. A key task ahead for media students is to sceptically assess these changes, particularly in an international context, rather than assuming particular stories about new media (based, for instance, on the digital cultures of the US or Europe, or indeed selective portrayals of new-technology adoption and use of any country) have general applicability. It is vital to enquire which particular ideas are associated with new technologies and whose interests are being served in their introduction and embedding in social life.

If a critical temper is crucial for pouring cold water on the overblown promises of new media technologies, it is even more necessary when scrutinizing heightened anxieties, full-blown fears and persistent moral panics. Key concerns in media still apply to new technologies, as we have seen. A great promise of new technology has been its decisive contribution to media diversity and freedom of the press. With the internet, many have pointed to the ease of use and low cost of publishing, allowing anyone who wishes to establish a press – at least wordpress in the shape of a blog – of their own. There are many important examples of such ventures, particularly in the many countries in the West where, especially in the wake of September 11, 2001, and the 'war on terror', press freedom is curtailed and extremely fraught. Yet, the power of media monopolies and corporations that dominate old media, plus new interests in old as well as new media (financial capital, venture capital, computer, internet and mobile companies) mean that genuine, lasting diversity of many aspects of media is a work in progress. On the one hand, search technologies greatly extend our access to news and information. It is possible now to bypass existing press and broadcasting outlets or supplement or supplant these with news aggregation, open news, etc. On the other hand, there remains a grey uniformity to the actual bulk of the news produced, circulated and consumed. The real work and economies of journalism might well be on the way to being shared, crowd-sourced or reinvented. However, the kind of journalism and news that media consumers are calling for can take much time, money, expertise and ongoing support to create and maintain.

New technologies also bring with them new media issues. Universal access, availability and use of new technologies become much more visible and pressing concerns. It is no longer simply a matter of ensuring universal service for those within a national territory in the West (whose citizens actually, in numeric terms, actually form the minority of the world population). Access is a vast problem for the global south (the majority world, in fact). Mobile-phone subscriptions worldwide are set to exceed the population of the world itself but this staggering statistic actually reveals little about the kinds of access to and use of this crucial new media technology that various populations, and differentiated groups within these populations, really afford and enjoy. Little is known about the actual media infrastructures that result from combinations of new technologies and old technologies. The same applies to media technologies that people own, rent, borrow, lend, modify, use, misuse or forget about. There are many assumptions embedded in the technologies themselves, and the official and unofficial discourses in which they acquire meaning, that bear little relationship to how technologies actually take shape on the ground, in the hands, hearts, minds and senses of their users.

One new concern for media students, organizations and regulators now is understanding the cultural politics that the technologies bring i.e., understanding the characteristics, affordances and cultures of digital networks and technologies. We need to examine the interconnections, compatibilities and interactions among various technologies and platforms, and how these fit into larger, reshuffled media and communication ecologies.

Another pressing concern is intellectual property – who owns, controls and regulates the sharing of ideas, to what ends and in whose interests. Intellectual property, in many ways, is to the present climate what media diversity was to twentieth-century media. At stake is how will we be able to gain access to the intellectual wealth of the digital networks that undergird, and indeed increasingly constitute, our media.

This is a complex, hard-fought battle over the countervailing desires, rights and responsibilities of users and citizens, authors and producers, technology manufacturers and media corporations.

In addition, we still have much to do in order to fathom the new kinds of communities, publics and relationships being created with technologies. New technologies, such as locative media, also greatly extend the boundaries previously believed to delineate and circumscribe media. So to people interested in studying and producing media, this signifies the need to return to older ideas of communication – to do with transport, for instance, or the role of cities – to understand phenomena such as the embedding of new media technologies in a range of aspects of everyday life, the public screens of contemporary, highly mediated cities, the role of new media in sustainability and the environment and emergent ecological cultures.

Suffice to say that these concerns, old and new, that new technologies elicit concerning the media will place even greater demands upon us as consumers, producers, students and researchers of media. Yet, to end on a hopeful note, the better prepared we are for an enthusiastic but critical engagement, the better chance we have to mindfully play a part in shaping technologies and the media for the betterment of all.

Bibliography

Abraham, R. (2007) 'Mobile Phones and Economic Development: Evidence from the Fishing Industry in India', *Information Technologies and International Development* vol. 4, pp. 5–17.

Abramson, A. (2003) *The History of Television, 1942 to 2000* (Jefferson, NC: McFarland & Co.).

Alasuutari, P. (ed.) (1999) *Rethinking the Media Audience: The New Agenda* (London and Thousand Oaks, CA: Sage).

Alcatel-Lucent (2009) *NBN TV Whitepaper* (Sydney: Alcatel-Lucent).

Aldrich, M. (1982) *Videotex, Key to the Wired City* (London: Quiller Press).

Allan, S. (2004) *News Culture* (2nd edn) (Maidenhead and New York: Open University Press).

Allan, S. (2006) *Online News: Journalism and the Internet* (Maidenhead: Open University Press).

Allan, S. and E. Thorsen (eds) (2009) *Citizen Journalism: Global Perspectives* (New York: Peter Lang).

Allen, M. (2008) 'Web 2.0: An Argument against Convergence', *First Monday* vol. 13 no. 3. Available at http://firstmonday.org/htbin/cgiwrap/bin/ojs/index.php/fm/rt/printerFriendly/2139/1946.

Allen, M. (2009) 'Tim O'Reilly and Web 2.0: The Economics of Memetic Liberty and Control', *Communications, Politics and Culture* vol. 42, pp. 6–23.

Anderson, B. (2006) *Imagined Communities: Reflections on the Origin and Spread of Nationalism* (London and New York: Verso).

Anderson, C. (2006) *The Long Tail: How Endless Choice Is Creating Unlimited Demand* (London: Random House).

Ang, I. (1991) *Desperately Seeking the Audience* (London and New York: Routledge).

Aspray, W. and P. E. Ceruzzi (2008) *The Internet and American Business* (Cambridge, MA: MIT Press)

Atton, C. (2004) *An Alternative Internet: Radical Media, Politics, and Creativity* (Edinburgh: Edinburgh University Press).

Atton, C. and J. F. Hamilton (2008) *Alternative Journalism* (London: Sage).

Ball, J. (2011) 'WikiLeaks Publishes Full Cache of Unredacted Cables', *Guardian*. Available at http://www.guardian.co.uk/media/2011/sep/02/wikileaks-publishes-cache-unredacted-cables.

Baltruschat, D. (2010) *Global Media Ecologies: Networked Production in Film and Television* (New York: Routledge).

Banet-Weiser, S., C. Chris and A. Freitas (eds) (2007) *Cable Visions: Television beyond Broadcasting* (New York: New York University Press).

Barlow, A. (2005) *The DVD Revolution: Movies, Culture, and Technology* (Westport, CT: Praeger).

Barlow, J. P. (1996) 'A Declaration of the Independence of Cyberspace'. Available at http://www.eff.org/~barlow/Declaration-Final.html.

Barsamian, D. (2002) *The Decline and Fall of Public Broadcasting* (2nd edn) (Cambridge, MA: South End Press).

Bartholomeusz, S. (2009) 'Will Conroy Kill Free TV?' *Business Spectator*. Available at http://www.businessspectator.com.au/bs.nsf/Article/Will-Conroy-kill-free-TV-pd20090921-W44XD?OpenDocument&src=kgb.

Baym, N. K. (2000) *Tune In, Log On: Soaps, Fandom, and Online Community* (Thousand Oaks, CA: Sage).

Baym, N. K. (2010) *Personal Connections in the Digital Age* (Cambridge: Polity).

BBC (2005) 'Building Public Value: Renewing the BBC for a Digital World'. Available at http://www.bbc.co.uk/aboutthebbc/purpose/charter/.

Bell, D. (1999) *The Coming of Post-Industrial Society: A Venture in Social Forecasting* (anniversary edn) (New York: Basic Books).

Bell, M. L. (2007) *Inventing Digital Television: The Inside Story of a Technology Revolution* (London: London Press).

Bender, W. (2002) 'Twenty Years of Personalization: All about the "Daily Me"' *Educause Review*, September/October, pp. 20–9.

Benkler, Y. (2006) *The Wealth of Networks: How Social Production Transforms Markets and Freedom* (New Haven, CT: Yale University Press).

Bennett, J. and T. Brown (eds) (2008) *Film and Television after DVD* (New York: Routledge).

Bennett, J. and N. Strange (eds) (2011) *Television as Digital Media* (Durham, NC: Duke University Press).

Berger, I. (1972) *Popular Mechanics* vol. 182, July, pp. 74–5.

Berker, T. (2006) *Domestication of Media and Technology* (Maidenhead: Open University Press).

Berkman Center for Internet and Society (ed.) (2010) *Next Generation Connectivity: A Review of Broadband Internet Transitions and Policy from around the World* (final report) (Boston, MA: Berkman Center, Harvard University).

Berners-Lee, T. and M. Fischetti (1999) *Weaving the Web: The Original Design and Ultimate Destiny of the World Wide Web by Its Inventor* (San Francisco, CA: Harper).

Beros, M. (2004) *Video-on-Demand: A False Dawn?* (Melbourne: RMIT Press).

Berry, J. P. (1987) *John F. Kennedy and the Media: The First Television President* (Lanham, MD: University Press of America).

Bijker, W. E., T. P. Hughes and T. J. Pinch (1987) *The Social Construction of Technological Systems: New Directions in the Sociology and History of Technology* (Cambridge, MA: MIT Press).

Bird, S. E. (ed.) (2010) *The Anthropology of News and Journalism: Global Perspectives* (Bloomington: Indiana University Press).

Blair, T. (2010) *A Journey: My Political Life* (New York: Knopf Doubleday).

Boczkowski, P. J. (2004a) *Digitizing the News: Innovation in Online Newspapers* (Cambridge, MA: MIT Press).

Boczkowski, P. J. (2004b) 'The Processes of Adopting Multimedia and Interactivity in Three Online Newsrooms', *Journal of Communication* vol. 54, pp. 197–213.

Boellstorff, T. (2008) *Coming of Age in Second Life: An Anthropologist Explores the Virtually Human* (Princeton, NJ: Princeton University Press).

Boler, M. (ed.) (2008) *Digital Media and Democracy: Tactics in Hard Times* (Cambridge, MA: MIT Press).

Bourne, C. P. and T. B. Hahn (2003) *A History of Online Information Services, 1963–1976* (Cambridge, MA: MIT Press).

Brophy, E. and G. de Peuter (2007) 'Immaterial Labor, Precarity, and Recomposition,' in C. McKercher and V. Mosco (eds), *Knowledge Workers in the Information Society* (Lanham, MD: Lexington Books).

Brown, A. and R. G. Picard (eds) (2005) *Digital Terrestrial Television in Europe* (Mahwah, NJ: Lawrence Erlbaum).

Brugger, N. (ed.) (2010) *Web History* (New York: Peter Lang).

Bruijn, M. E., F. Nyamnjoh and I. Brinkman (2009) *Mobile Phones: The New Talking Drums of Everyday Africa* (Bamenda, Cameroon: Langaa Publishers).

Bruns, A. (2005) *Gatewatching: Collaborative Online News Production* (New York: Peter Lang).

Bruns, A. (2008) *Blogs, Wikipedia, Second Life, and Beyond: From Production to Produsage* (New York: Peter Lang).

Bruns, A. and J. Jacobs (eds) (2006) *Uses of Blogs* (New York: Peter Lang).

Brunsdon, C. and D. Morley (1978) *Everyday Television: 'Nationwide'* (London: BFI).

Bulkeley, W. M. (2010) 'Social TV. Relying on Relationships to Rebuild TV Audiences', *MIT Technology Review*, TR10. Available at http://www.technology review.com/communications/25084/?a=f.

Burgess, J. and J. Green (2009) *YouTube: Online Video and Participatory Culture* (Cambridge and Malden, MA: Polity Press).

Burns, M. (2008) *ABC Online: Becoming the ABC* (Saarbrücken: Verlag Dr. Muller).

Burns, M. and N. Brügger (eds) (2012) *Histories of Public Service Broadcasters on the Web* (New York: Peter Lang).

Bury, R. (2005) *Cyberspaces of Their Own: Female Fandoms Online* (New York: Peter Lang).

Cailliau, R. (2000) *How the Web Was Born: The Story of the World Wide Web* (New York: Oxford University Press).

Carpentier, N. and B. De Cleen (2008) *Participation and Media Production: Critical Reflections on Content Creation* (Newcastle: Cambridge Scholars Press).

Carr-Saunders, A. M. and P. A. Wilson (1933) *The Professions* (Oxford: Clarendon Press).

Castillo, M. (2011) 'Bodies Hanging from Bridge in Mexico Are Warning to Social Media Users', *CCN.com*, 15 September. Available at http://edition.cnn.com/2011/WORLD/americas/09/14/mexico.violence/index.html?hpt=hp_t2.

Castranova, E. (2005) *Synthetic Worlds: The Business and Culture of Online Games* (Chicago, IL: University of Chicago Press).

Cave, M. and K. Nakamura (eds) (2006) *Digital Broadcasting: Policy and Practice in the Americas, Europe and Japan* (Cheltenham: Edward Elgar).

Cawley, A. (2008) 'News Production in an Irish Online Newsroom: Practice, Process, and Culture', in C. Paterson and D. Domingo (eds), *Making Online News: The Ethnography of New Media Production* (New York: Peter Lang), pp. 45–60.

Chadwick, A. and P. N. Howard (eds) (2008) *Routledge Handbook of Internet Politics* (New York: Routledge).

Clarke, R., G. Dempsey, O. C. Nee and R. F. O'Connor (1998) 'A Primer on Internet Technology', 15 February. Available at http://www.rogerclarke.com/II/IPrimer.html.

Clements, C. (2008) 'Can TiVo Take on Foxtel IQ?', *news.com.au*, 8 October. Available at http://www.news.com.au/technology/can-tivo-take-on-foxtel-iq/story-e6frfro0-1111117688358.

Clode, G. (2010a) 'The Cable Story'. Available at http://www.rediffusion.info/cablestory.html.

Clode, G. (2010b) 'Remembering Rediffusion Ltd'. Available at http://www.rediffusion.info.

Coleman, S. (2009) *The Internet and Democratic Citizenship: Theory, Practice and Policy* (Cambridge and New York: Cambridge University Press).

Collins, R. (2010) 'Public Service Broadcasting: Yesterday, Today and Tomorrow'. Available at http://www.opendemocracy.net/ourkingdom/richard-collins/public-service-broadcasting-yesterday-today-and-tomorrow.

Compton, J. R. (2010) 'Newspapers, Labor and the Flux of Economic Uncertainty', in S. Allan (ed.), *Routledge Companion to News and Journalism* (London and New York: Routledge), pp. 591–601.

Consalvo, M. and S. Paasonen (eds) (2002) *Women and Everyday Uses of the Internet* (New York: Peter Lang).

Council of the European Communities (EC) (1989) 'Television without Frontiers', Council Directive, 89/552/EEC, 3 October. Available at: http://eur-lex.europa.eu/LexUriServ/site/en/consleg/1989/L/01989L0552-19970730-en.pdf.

Crandall, R. W. (2005) *Competition and Chaos: U.S. Telecommunications since the 1996 Telecom Act* (Washington, DC: Brookings Institution).

Crawford, K. (2009) 'These Foolish Things: On Intimacy and Insignificance in Mobile Media', in G. Goggin and L. Hjorth (eds), *Mobile Technologies: From Telecommunications to Media* (New York: Routledge), pp. 250–63.

Crisell, A. (2006) *A Study of Modern Television: Thinking inside the Box* (Basingstoke: Palgrave Macmillan).

Cryle, D. (1997) *Disreputable Profession: Journalists and Journalism in Colonial Australia* (Rockhampton, Qld: CQU Press).

Curran, J. and J. Seaton (2010) *Power without Responsibility: Press, Broadcasting and the Internet in Britain* (7th edn) (London and New York: Routledge).

Dahlgren, P. (2009) *Media and Political Engagement: Citizens, Communication and Democracy* (Cambridge: Cambridge University Press).

David, M. (2010) *Peer to Peer and the Music Industry: The Criminalization of Sharing* (Los Angeles, CA and London: Sage).

De Angelis, M. (2007) *The Beginning of History: Value Struggles and Global Capital* (London: Pluto Press).

Department for Business, Innovation and Skills (BIS) and the Department for Culture, Media and Sport (DCMS) (2009) *Digital Britain*. Final Report (Norwich: TSO).

Department for Culture, Media and Sport (DCMS) (2009) *Digital Britain: Final Report* (London: British Parliament).

Department for Culture Media and Sport (2006) *Broadcasting: Copy of Royal Charter for the Continuance of the British Broadcasting Corporation* (London: HMSO).

Deuze, M. (2003) 'The Web and Its Journalisms: Considering the Consequences of Different Types of Newsmedia Online', *New Media and Society* vol. 3, pp. 205–30.

Deuze, M. (2007) *Media Work* (Cambridge: Polity Press).

Deuze, M. and L. Fortunati (2010) 'Journalism without Journalists: On the Power Shift from Journalists to Employers and Audiences', in G. Meikle and G. Redden (eds), *News Online: Transformations and Continuities* (New York: Palgrave Macmillan), pp. 164–77.

Domingo, D. and C. Paterson (eds) (2011) *Making Online News: Newsroom Ethnographies in the Second Decade of Internet Journalism* (New York: Peter Lang).

Domscheit-Berg, D. (2011) *Inside WikiLeaks: My Time with Julian Assange at the World's Most Dangerous Website* (New York: Crown).

Donner, J. (2009) 'Mobile Media on Low-Cost Handsets: The Resiliency of Text Messaging among Small Enterprises in India (and Beyond)', in G. Goggin and L. Hjorth (eds), *Mobile Technologies: From Telecommunications to Media* (New York: Routledge), pp. 93–104.

Downey, G. J. (2008) *Closed Captioning: Subtitling, Stenography, and the Digital Convergence of Text with Television* (Baltimore, MD: Johns Hopkins University Press).

Ducheneaut, N. M., L. Oehlberg, R. J. Moore, J. D. Thornton and E. Nickell (2008) 'Social TV: Designing for Distributed, Sociable Television Viewing', *International Journal of Human–Computer Interaction* vol. 24, pp. 136–54.

Dunn, A. (2004) 'From Quasi to Fully: On Journalism as a Profession', *Australian Journalism Review* vol. 26, pp. 21–30.

Dwyer, T. (2010) *Media Convergence* (Maidenhead: Open University Press).

Eble, K. and T. Gunnel (2006) 'Networking Community Media: Web Radio as a Participatory Medium', in P. W. Lewis and S. Jones (eds) (Cresskill, NJ: Hampton Press).

Ekine, S. (ed.) (2010) *Mobile Phone Activism in Africa* (Cape Town: Pambazuka).

Elstein, D. (2008) 'How to Fund Public Service Content in the Digital Age', in T. Gardam and D. A. L. Levy (eds), *The Price of Plurality: Choice, Diversity and Broadcasting Institutions in the Digital Age* (Oxford: Reuters Institute for the Study of Journalism, Oxford University), pp. 86–90.

Ettema, J. S. and T. L. Glasser (1998) *Custodians of Conscience: Investigative Journalism and Public Virtue* (New York: Columbia University Press).

Fedida, S. and R. Malik (1979) *Viewdata Revolution* (London: Associated Business Press).

Fenton, N. (2010a) 'Drowning or Waving? New Media, Journalism and Democracy', in N. Fenton (ed.), *New Media, Old News: Journalism and Democracy in the Digital Age* (Los Angeles, CA: Sage), pp. 3–16.

Fenton, N. (ed.) (2010b) *New Media, Old News: Journalism and Democracy in the Digital Age* (Los Angeles, CA: Sage).

Flew, T. (2008) *New Media: An Introduction* (Melbourne: Oxford University Press).

Flew, T. (2011) *Creative Industries: Culture and Policy* (Thousand Oaks, CA: Sage).

Flichy, P. (2007) *The Internet imaginaire* (Cambridge, MA: MIT Press).

Friedman, T. (2005) *Electric Dreams: Computers in American Culture* (New York: New York University Press).

Furht, B. and S. Ahson (eds) (2008) *Handbook of Mobile Broadcasting DVB-H, DMB, iSDB-T, and Mediaflo* (Boca Raton, FL: Auerbach).

Gane, N. and D. Beer (2008) *New Media: The Key Concepts* (Oxford and New York: Berg).

Ganley, G. D. (1992) *The Exploding Political Power of Personal Media* (Norwood, NJ: Ablex).

Gardam, T. (2008) 'The Purpose of Plurality', in T. Gardam and D. A. L. Levy (eds), *The Price of Plurality: Choice, Diversity and Broadcasting Institutions in the Digital Age* (Oxford: Reuters Institute for the Study of Journalism, Oxford University), pp. 11–21.

Gardam, T. and D. A. L. Levy (eds) (2008) *The Price of Plurality: Choice, Diversity and Broadcasting Institutions in the Digital Age* (Oxford: Reuters Institute for the Study of Journalism, Oxford University).

Gauntlett, D. and R. Horsley (eds) (2004) *Web.studies* (2nd edn) (London: Arnold).

Genensky, S. M. *et al.* (1968) *A Closed Circuit TV System for the Visually Handicapped* (Santa Monica, CA: Rand).

Gerbarg, D. and E. Noam (2004) 'Introduction', in E. Noam, J. Groebel and D. Gerbarg (eds), *Internet Television* (Mahwah, NJ: Lawrence Erlbaum).

Gibson, J. J. (1977) 'The Theory of Affordances', in R. E. Shaw and J. Bransford (eds), *Perceiving, Acting, and Knowing: Toward an Ecological Psychology* (Hillsdale, NJ: Lawrence Erlbaum), pp. 67–82.

Gibson, W. (1984) *Neuromancer* (New York: Ace Books).

Gibson, W. (1986) *Burning Chrome* (New York: Arbor House).

Gillmor, D. (2004) *We the Media: Grassroots Journalism by the People, for the People* (Sebastopol, CA: O'Reilly Media).

Gillmor, D. (2011) 'The *New York Times* Paywall: The Faint Scent of Success', *Guardian.co.uk*, 3 August. Available at http://www.guardian.co.uk/comment isfree/cifamerica/2011/aug/03/new-york-times-paywal.

Gitlin, T. (1994) *Inside Prime Time* (rev. edn) (London: Routledge).

Given, J. (2003) *Turning Off the Television: Broadcasting's Uncertain Future* (Sydney: UNSW Press).

Glasner, J. (2004) 'Wikipedia Creators Move into News', *Wired.com*, 29 November. Available at http://www.wired.com/culture/lifestyle/news/2004/11/65819.

Glasser, T. L. (ed.) (1999) *The Idea of Public Journalism* (New York: Guildford Press).

Goggin, G. (2011a) 'Global Internets: Media Research in the New World', in I. Volkmer (ed.), *Handbook of Global Media Research* (Malden, MA: Wiley-Blackwell), forthcoming.

Goggin, G. (2011b) *Global Mobile Media* (London and New York: Routledge).

Goggin, G. (2011c) 'Ubiquitous Apps: Politics of Openness in Global Mobile Cultures', *Digital Creativity* vol. 22, pp. 147–57.

Goggin, G. and L. Hjorth (2009) 'Waiting to Participate: Introduction', *Communication, Politics and Culture* vol. 42, pp. 1–5.

Goggin, G. and C. Newell (2003) *Digital Disability: The Social Construction of Disability in New Media* (Lanham, MD: Rowman and Littlefield).

Golding, P, and G. Murdock (2001) 'Digital Divides: Communications Policy and Its Contradictions', *New Economy* vol. 8, pp. 110–15.

Graham, F. (2011) 'Beyond the Couch: TV Goes Social, Goes Everywhere', *BBC News*, 16 September. Available at http://www.bbc.co.uk/news/business-14921491.

Graziplene, L. R. (2000) *Teletext: Its Promise and Demise* (Cranbury, NJ and London: Associated University Presses).

Greenberg, A. (2010) 'Meet the New Public Face of WikiLeaks: Kristinn Hrafnsson', *Forbes*, 17 December. Available at http://www.forbes.com/sites/andygreenberg/2010/12/07/meet-the New-Public-Face-of-wikiLeaks-kristinn-hrafnsson/.

Greif, H., L. Hjorth, A. Lasén and C. Lobet-Maris (2011) *Cultures of Participation* (New York: Peter Lang).

Grint, K. and S. Woolgar (1997) *The Machine at Work: Technology, Work and Organization* (Cambridge: Polity Press).

Gripsrud, J. (ed.) (2010) *Relocating Television: Television in the Digital Context* (London and New York: Routledge).

Grossman, L. (2010) 'Person of the Year 2010: Mark Zuckerberg', *Time*, 15 December. Available at http://www.time.com/time/specials/packages/article/0,28804,2036683_2037183,00.html.

Guardian (2008) 'History of the *Guardian*'. Available at http://www.guardian.co.uk/gnm-archive/2002/jun/06/1.

Guardian (2009) 'Rupert Murdoch's Plans for an Ebook Reader', *PDA: The Digital Content Blog*, 7 May 2009. Available at http://www.guardian.co.uk/media/pda/2009/may/07/rupert-murdoch-news-corporation.

Guardian (2010) 'Afghanistan War Logs: How the *Guardian* Got the Story', 25 July. Available at http://www.guardian.co.uk/world/2010/jul/25/afghanistan-war-logs-explained-video.

Guardian (2011) 'After Hacking?: How Can the Press Restore Trust'. Available at http://www.guardian.co.uk/hacking-debate.

Haddon, L. (2006) 'The Contribution of Domestication Research to In-Home Computing and Media Consumption', *Information Society* vol. 22, pp. 195–203.

Haddon, L., E. Mante, B. Sapio, K.-H. Kommonen, L. Fortunati and A. Kant (eds) (2005) *Everyday Innovators: Researching the Role of Users in Shaping ICTs* (London: Springer).

Harper, C. (1999) *And That's the Way It Will Be: News and Information in a Digital World* (New York and London: New York University Press).

Hartley, J. (ed.) (2005) *Creative Industries* (Malden, MA and Oxford: Blackwell).

Hartley, J. (2009) *The Uses of Digital Literacy* (Brisbane: University of Queensland Press).

Hauben, M. and R. Hauben (1997) *Netizens: On the History and Impact of Usenet and the Internet* (Los Alamitos, CA: IEEE Computer Society Press).

Hawk, B., D. M. Rieder and O. O. Oviedo (eds) (2008) *Small Tech: The Culture of Digital Tools* (Minneapolis: University of Minnesota Press).

Hernandez, D. (2011) 'Veracruz Panic Started before 'Terrorist' Tweets, Reports Say', *LA Times*, 9 September. Available at http://latimesblogs.latimes.com/laplaza/2011/09/twitter-mexico-veracruz-details-confusion-rumor-precedents.html.

Hill, A. and R. C. Allen (eds) (2004) *The Television Studies Reader* (New York: Routledge).

Hillis, K. (2009) *Online a Lot of the Time: Ritual, Fetish, Sign* (Durham, NC: Duke University Press).

Hillis, K. and M. Petit (eds) (2006) *Everyday eBay: Culture, Collecting, and Desire* (New York: Routledge).

Hindman, M. (2009) *The Myth of Digital Democracy* (Princeton, NJ: Princeton University Press).

Hjorth, L. (2009) *Mobile Media in the Asia-Pacific: Gender and the Art of Being Mobile* (London and New York: Routledge).

Hollander, R. S. (1985) *Video Democracy: The Vote-from-Home Revolution* (Mt Airy, MD: Lomond).

Hollins, T. (1984) *Beyond Broadcasting: Into the Cable Age* (London: BFI).

House of Representatives Standing Committee on Communications (2006) *Digital Television – Who's Buying It?: Inquiry into the Uptake of Digital Television in Australia* (Canberra: Parliament of Australia).

Howett, D. (2006) *Television Innovations: 50 years of Development* (Devon: Kelly Publications).

Huffington, A. (2009) 'The Paywall Is History', *Guardian*, 11 May. Available at http://www.guardian.co.uk/commentisfree/2009/may/11/newspapers-web-media-pay-wall?INTCMP=SRCH.

Huffington Post (2010) 'Norway's Stranded Prime Minister Uses iPad to Govern from U.S.', 15 April. Available at http://www.huffingtonpost.com/2010/04/15/norways-stranded-prime-mi_n_539938.html.

Hughes, T. P. (1987) 'The Evolution of Large Technological Systems', in W. E. Bijker, T. P. Hughes and T. J. Pinch (eds), *The Social Construction of Technological Systems: New Directions in the Sociology and History of Technology* (Cambridge, MA: MIT Press), pp. 51–82.

Iggers, J. (1998) *Good News, Bad News: Journalism Ethics and the Public Interest* (Boulder, CO: Westview Press).

Index on Censorship (2008) 'Winners of Index on Censorship Freedom of Expression Awards announced'. Available at http://www.indexoncensorship.org/2008/04/winners-of-index-on-censorship-freedom-of-expression-award-announced/.

Intel (2010) 'Smart TV'. Available at http://www.intel.com/inside/smarttv/.

International Telecommunications Union (ITU) (2010) 'Key Global Telecom Indicators for the World Telecommunication Service Sector'. Available at http://www.itu.int/ITU-D/ict/statistics/at_glance/KeyTelecom.html.

Jenkins, H. (2006) *Fans, Bloggers, and Gamers: Exploring Participatory Culture* (New York: New York University Press).

Jones, S. E. (2006) *Against Technology: From the Luddites to Neo-Luddism* (New York: Routledge).

Jouët, J., P. Flichy and P. Beaud (eds) (1991) *European Telematics: The Emerging Economy of Words* (Amsterdam and New York: North Holland).

Joyce, M. (2007) *The Citizen Journalism Web Site 'OhmyNews' and the 2002 South Korean Presidential Election* (Cambridge, MA: Berkman Center for Internet and Society, Harvard University).

Kahn, R. and D. Kellner (2008) 'Technopolitics, Blogs, and Emergent Media Ecologies: A Critical/Reconstructive Approach', in B. Hawk, D. M. Rieder and O. O. Oviedo (eds), *Small Tech: The Culture of Digital Tools* (Minneapolis: University of Minnesota Press), pp. 22–37.

Kelly, K. (1998) *New Rules for the New Economy: 10 Radical Strategies for a Connected World* (New York: Viking Press).

Kennedy, D. (2010) 'Why WikiLeaks Turned to the Press', *Guardian*, 27 July. Available at http://www.guardian.co.uk/commentisfree/cifamerica/ 2010/jul/27/why-wikiLeaks-turned-to-press.

Kim, E. G. and J. W. Hamilton (2006) 'Capitulation to Capital? OhmyNews as Alternative Media', *Media Culture Society* vol. 28, pp. 541–60.

Koch, C. (1998) *Video on Demand: Television for a New Millennium* (Norderstedt: GRIN Verlag).

Kompare, D. (2005) *Rerun Nation: How Repeats Invented American Television* (New York and London: Routledge).

Kücklich, J. (2005) 'Precarious Playbour: Modders and the Digital Games Industry', *Fibreculture Journal* vol. 5. Available at http://journal.fibreculture. org/issue5/kucklich.html.

Küng, L., R. G. Picard and R. Towse (eds) (2008) *The Internet and Mass Media* (Los Angeles, CA: Sage).

Kyrish, S. (1994) 'Here Comes the Revolution – Again: Evaluating Predictions for the Information Superhighway', *Media International Australia* vol. 74, pp. 5–14.

LA Times (2010) 'News Corp. Plans National Newspaper for Tablet Computers and Cellphones', *Los Angeles Times*, 13 August. Available at http://articles. latimes.com/2010/aug/13/business/la-fi-ct-newscorp-20100813.

Lampland, M. and S. L. Star (eds) (2009) *Standards and Their Stories: How Quantifying, Classifying, and Formalizing Practices Shape Everyday Life* (Ithaca, NY: Cornell University Press).

Latour, B. (1996) *Aramis, or, The Love of Technology* (trans. C. Porter) (Cambridge, MA: Harvard University Press).

Latour, B. (2004) *The Politics of Nature: How to Bring the Sciences into Democracy* (Cambridge, MA: Harvard University Press).

Latour, B. (2005) *Reassembling the Social: An Introduction to Actor-Network-Theory* (Oxford: Clarendon Press).

Law, J. and J. Hassard (1999) *Actor Network Theory and After* (Oxford: Blackwell).

Lazzarato, M. (1996) 'Immaterial Labor', in P. Virno and M. Hardt (eds), *Radical Thought in Italy: A Potential Politics* (Minneapolis: University of Minnesota Press), pp. 133–47.

Lazzarato, M. (1997) *Lavoro immateriale [Immaterial Labour]* (Verona: Ombre Corte).

Leadbeater, C. (2004) *The Pro-Am Revolution: How Enthusiasts Are Changing Our Economy and Society* (London: Demos).

Lecesse, M. (2009 'Online Information Sources of Political Blogs', *Journalism and Mass Communication Quarterly* vol. 86, pp. 578–93.

Leigh, D. and L. Harding (2011) *WikiLeaks: Inside Julian Assange's War on Secrecy* (London: Guardian Books).

LeMasurier, M. (2012) 'Independent Magazines and the Rejuvenation of Print', *International Journal of Cultural Studies*, forthcoming.

Lindgren, S. and R. Lundström (2011) 'Pirate Culture and Hacktivist Mobilization: The Cultural and Social Protocols of #WikiLeaks on Twitter', *New Media and Society*, 27 June, DOI: 10.1177/1461444811414833.

Lister, M., J. Dovey, S. Giddings, I. Grant and K. Kelly (2009) *New Media: A Critical Introduction* (London and New York: Routledge).

Livingstone, S. M. and L. A. Lievrouw (eds) (2009) *New Media* (London: Sage).

Lobato, R. (2010) 'Creative Industries and Informal Economies: Lessons from Nollywood', *International Journal of Cultural Studies* vol. 13, pp. 337–54.

Loewenstein, A. (2008) *The Blogging Revolution* (Melbourne: Melbourne University Publishing).

Löfgren, O. and R. Willim (eds) (2005) *Magic, Culture and the New Economy* (Oxford and New York: Berg).

Loomis, D. and P. Meyer (2000) 'Opinion without Polls: Finding a Link between Corporate Culture and Public Journalism', *International Journal of Public Opinion Research* vol. 12, pp. 276–84.

Lopez-Pumarejo, T. (1987) *Aproximación a la Telenovela: Dallas, Dinasty, Falcon Crest* (Madrid: Catedra).

Lotz, A. D. (2007) *The Television Will Be Revolutionized* (New York: New York University Press).

Lotz, A. D. (2009) *Beyond Prime Time: Television Programming in the Post-Network Era* (New York: Routledge).

Lovink, G. (2003) *My First Recession: Critical Internet Culture in Transition* (Rotterdam: V2_Publishing/NAI Publishers).

Lovink, G. (2008) *Zero Comments: Blogging and Critical Internet Culture* (New York: Routledge).

Lull, J. (1990) *Inside Family Viewing: Ethnographic Research on Television's Audiences* (London: Routledge).

Mabbott-Athique, A. (2008) 'The Global Dynamics of Indian Media Piracy: Export Markets, Playback Media and the Informal Economy', *Media Culture and Society* vol. 30, pp. 699–717.

MacKenzie, D. A. and J. Wajcman (1985) *The Social Shaping of Technology: How the Refrigerator Got Its Hum* (Milton Keynes and Philadelphia, PA: Open University Press).

Maddox, G. and D. Court (1989) *The Home Video Industry Report* (Sydney: Australian Film Commission).

Malaby, T. M. (2009) *Making Virtual Worlds: Linden Lab and Second Life* (Ithaca, NY: Cornell University Press).

Marchand, M. (1987) *La Grande Aventure du Minitel* (Paris: Larousse).

Marchart, O. (2007) *The Rise of the Informal Media: How Search Engines, Weblogs and YouTube Change Public Opinion* (Rotterdam: NAI).

Marcus, A., A. Cereijo Roibas and R. Sala (eds) (2010) *Mobile TV: Customizing Content and Experience: Mobile Storytelling, Creation and Sharing* (London and New York: Springer).

Martin, F. (2004) 'Net Worth: The Unlikely Rise of ABC Online', in G. Goggin (ed.), *Virtual Nation: The Internet in Australia* (Sydney: University of New South Wales Press).

Mayne, A. J. (1982) *The Videotex Revolution* (Fareham: October Press).

Mazziotti, N. (2006) *Telenovela, Industria y Prácticas Sociales* (Bogotá, Colombia: Grupo Editorial Norma).

McDonald, P. (2007) *Video and DVD Industries* (London: BFI).

McLuhan, M. (1964) *Understanding Media: The Extensions of Man* (London: Routledge & Kegan Paul).

McLuhan, M. (1967) *The Medium Is the Massage* (London: Allen Lane).

McNair, B. (2006) *Cultural Chaos: Journalism, News, and Power in a Globalised World* (New York: Routledge).

McNair, B. (2009) *News and Journalism in the UK* (5th edn) (London and New York: Routledge).

Media Entertainment and Arts Alliance (MEAA) (2008) *Life in the Clickstream: The Future of Journalism* (Sydney: MEAA).

Meikle, G. (2002) *Future Active: Media Activism and the Internet* (New York: Routledge).

Meikle, G. and G. Redden (eds) (2010) *News Online: Transformations and Continuity* (Basingstoke: Palgrave Macmillan).

Meikle, G. and S. Young (2007) 'Beyond Broadcasting: TV for the Twenty-First Century', *Media International Australia* vol. 126, pp. 67–70.

Merrill Lynch (2009) *The NBN: What Does It Mean for TV?* (Sydney: Merrill Lynch).

Messner, M. and M. W. Distaso, (2008) 'The Source Cycle: How Traditional Media and Weblogs Use Each Other as Sources', *Journalism Studies* vol. 8, pp. 447–63.

Meyer, B. M. (ed.) (2009) *Aesthetic Formations: Media, Religion, and the Senses (*New York: Palgrave Macmillan).

Meyer, P. (2004) *The Vanishing Newspaper: Saving Journalism in the Information Age* (2nd edn) (Columbia: University of Missouri Press).

Meyers, G. (2010) *Discourse of Blogs and Wikis* (London and New York: Continuum).

Miller, N. and R. Allen (1995) *The Post-Broadcasting Age: New Technologies, New Communities: Papers from the 25th and 26th University of Manchester Broadcasting Symposia*, Luton.

Minoli, D. (1995) *Video Dialtone Technology: Digital Video over ADSL, HFC, FTTC, and ATM* (New York: McGraw-Hill).

Molloy, J. and C. Boyle (2010) 'Stephen Colbert, Jon Stewart "Rally to Restore Sanity and/or Fear" Draws Thousands of New Yorkers,' *New York Times*, 30 October. Available at http://www.nydailynews.com/news/politics/ 2010/10/ 30/2010-10-30_thousands_of_new_yorkers_drawn_to_ stephen_colbert_ jon_ stewart_rally_to_restore_s.html#ixzz16ZEJKftE.

Moran, A. (2009) *New Flows in Global TV* (Bristol and Chicago, IL: Intellect).

Moran, J. M. (2002) *There's No Place Like Home Video* (Minneapolis: University of Minnesota Press).

Morley, D. (1980) *The Nationwide Audience: Structure and Decoding* (London: BFI).

Morley, D. (1992) *Television, Audiences, and Cultural Studies* (London and New York: Routledge).

Mosco, V. and C. McKercher (2008) *The Laboring of Communication: Will Knowledge Workers of the World Unite?* (Lanham, MD: Lexington Books).

Mullan, B. (1997) *Consuming Television: Television and Its Audience* (Oxford and Cambridge, MA: Blackwell).

Mullen, M. G. (2008) *Television in the Multichannel Age: A Brief History of Cable Television* (Malden, MA: Blackwell).

Negri, A. (2008) *Empire and Beyond* (trans. E. Emery) (Cambridge: Polity Press).

Negroponte, N. (1995) *Being Digital* (New York: Knopf).

New York Times (2009) 'A New Way to Take Your News with You on the iPhone and iPod Touch'. Available at http://www.nytimes.com/services/mobile/iphone.html.

Nguyen, A. (2010) 'Marrying the Professional to the Amateur: Strategies and Implications of the OhMyNews Model', in G. Meikle and G. Redden (eds), *News Online: Transformations and Continuities* (Basingstoke and New York, Palgrave Macmillan), pp. 195–209.

Nielsen, R. K. and D. A. L. Levy (2010a) 'The Changing Business of Journalism and Its Implications for Democracy', in R. K. Nielsen and D. A. L. Levy (eds), *The Changing Business of Journalism and Its Implications for Democracy* (Oxford: Reuters Institute for the Study of Journalism, Oxford University), pp. 3–16.

Nielsen, R. K. and D. A. L. Levy (2010b) 'Which Way for the Business of Journalism?', in R. K. Nielsen and D. A. L. Levy (eds), *The Changing Business of Journalism and Its Implications for Democracy* (Oxford: Reuters Institute for the Study of Journalism, Oxford University), pp. 135–47.

Nightingale, V. (ed.) (2011) *The Handbook of Media Audiences* (New York: Wiley-Blackwell).

Noam, E. and L. M. Pupillo (2008) *Peer-to-Peer Video the Economics, Policy, and Culture of Today's New Mass Medium* (Dordrecht: Springer).

North, L. (2009) *The Gendered Newsroom: How Journalists Experience the Changing World of Media* (Cresskill, NJ: Hampton Press).

Nuechterlein, J. E. and P. J. Weiser (2005) *Digital Crossroads: American Telecommunications Policy in the Internet Age* (Cambridge, MA: MIT Press).

O'Neill, B. (ed.) (2010) *Digital Radio in Europe: Technologies, Industries and Cultures* (Bristol: Intellect).

O'Regan, M. (2000) 'The Outlook for Public Broadcasting, Is It Bright or Bleak?', part 2, *Media Report*, ABC Radio, 12 October. Available at http://www.abc.net.au/rn/talks/8.30/mediarpt/stories/s198700.htm.

O'Reilly, T. (2005) 'What Is Web 2.0: Design Patterns and Business Models for the Next Generation of Software', 30 September. Available at http://www.oreilly.com/pub/a/oreilly/tim/news/2005/09/30/what-is-web-20.html.

OECD (1988) *New Telecommunications Services: Videotex Development Strategies* (Paris: OECD).

OECD (2007) *Participative Web: User-Generated Content* (Paris: OECD).

OMNI (OhmyNewsInternational) (2010) 'OMNI's New Approach to Citizen Journalism', 8 January. Available at http://english.ohmynews.com.

Organization for Economic Cooperation and Development (OECD) (1998) *France's Experience with the Minitel: Lessons for Electronic Commerce over the Internet* (Paris: OECD).

Örnebring, H. (2010) 'Reassessing Journalism as a Profession', in S. Allan (ed.), *Routledge Companion to News and Journalism* (London and New York: Routledge).

Oudshoorn, N. and T. Pinch (eds) (2003) *How Users Matter: The Co-Construction of Users and Technologies* (Cambridge, MA: MIT Press).

Overholser, G. (2006) *On Behalf of Journalism: A Manifesto for Change* (Philadelphia, PA: Annenberg Public Policy Centre, University of Philadelphia).

Owen, B. M. (1999) *The Internet Challenge to Television* (Cambridge, MA: Harvard University Press).

Oxford English Dictionary (OED) (2010) 'Technology' (2nd edn) (Oxford: Oxford University Press).

Paasonen, S. (2009) 'What Cyberspace? Traveling Concepts in Internet Research', in G. Goggin and M. McLelland (eds), *Internationalizing Internet Studies* (New York: Routledge), pp. 18–31.

Paterson, C. and D. Domingo (eds) (2008) *Making Online News: The Ethnography of Media Production* (New York: Peter Lang).

Patrick, P. (2008) *Blue Skies: A History of Cable Television* (Philadelphia, PA: Temple University Press).

Pavlik, J. (2001) *Journalism and New Media* (New York: Columbia University Press).

Pavlik, J. V. (2008) *Media in the Digital Age* (New York: Columbia University Press).

Pavlik, J. V. and S. McIntosh (2011) *Converging Media: A New Introduction to Mass Communication* (Oxford: Oxford University Press).

Penttinen, J. (ed.) (2009) *The DVB-H Handbook: The Functioning and Planning of Mobile TV* (Chichester: John Wiley).

Perlmutter, D. D. (2008) *Blogwars* (New York: Oxford University Press).

Petros, I. and P. Iosifidis (2007) *Public Television in the Digital Era: Technological Challenges and New Strategies for Europe* (Basingstoke and New York: Palgrave Macmillan).

Pew Centre (2011) 'Publications on News Media'. Available at http://pewresearch.org/topics/newsmedia.

Pilkington, E. (2010) 'Rupert Murdoch 'to Launch US Digital Newspaper', *Guardian.co.uk*. Available at http://www.guardian.co.uk/media/2010/aug/2013/rupert-murdoch-us-digital-newspaper.

Poindexter, P. M., S. Meraz and A. S. Weiss (2008) *Women, Men, and News: Divided and Disconnected in the News Media Landscape* (New York and London: Routledge).

Pool, I. de S. (1973). *Talking Back: Citizen Feedback and Cable Technology* (Cambridge, MA: MIT Press).

Poynter Institute (2001) *Behind the Scenes: How Foundations Have Quietly Seized a Role in Journalism, Commissioning Content* (St Petersburg, FL: Poynter Institute).

Preston, P. (2011) 'A Paywall That Pays? Only in America', *The Observer*, 7 August. Available at http://www.guardian.co.uk/media/2011/aug/07/paywall-that-pays-only-in-america?INTCMP=SRCH.

Price, M. E. and J. Wicklein (1972) *Cable Television: A Guide for Citizen Action* (Philadelphia, PA: Pilgrim Press).

Raboy, M. (ed.) (1995) *Public Broadcasting for the 21st Century* (Luton: University of Luton Press).

Rettberg, J. W. (2008) *Blogging* (Cambridge and Malden, MA: Polity Press).

Rheingold, H. (1993) *The Virtual Community: Homesteading on the Electronic Frontier* (Reading, MA: Addison-Wesley).

Rheingold, H. (2002) *Smartmobs: The Next Social Revolution* (Cambridge, MA: Basic Books).

Rogers, E. M. (1995) *Diffusion of Innovations* (New York: Free Press).

Romano, A. (2010) *International Journalism and Democracy: Civic Engagement Models from around the World* (New York: Routledge).

Rosen, J. (1999) *What Are Journalists For?* (New Haven, CT: Yale University Press).

Rosen, J. (2005) 'Laying the Newspaper Gently Down to Die', 29 March. Available at http://archive.pressthink.org/2005/03/29/nwsp_dwn.html.

Rosen, J. (2006) 'The People Formerly Known as the Audience', 27 June. Available at http://archive.pressthink.org/2006/06/27/ppl_frmr.html#more.

Rosen, J. (2008) 'Migration Point for the Press Tribe', 26 June. Available at http://archive.pressthink.org/2008/06/26/pdf.html.

Rosen, J. (2010) 'The Journalists Formerly Known as the Media: My Advice to the Next Generation', 6 September. Available at http://jayrosen.posterous.com/the-journalists-formerly-known-as-the-media-m.

Ross, A. (2005) 'Technology', in T. Bennett, L. Grossberg and M. Morris (eds), *New Keywords: A Revised Vocabulary of Culture and Society* (Malden, MA: Blackwell), pp. 342–4.

Ross, A. (2009) *Nice Work If You Can Get It: Life and Labor in Precarious Times* (New York: New York University Press).

Ross, S. M. (2008) *Beyond the Box: Television and the Internet* (Malden, MA: Blackwell).

Russell, A. and N. Echchaibi (eds) (2009) *International Blogging: Identity, Politics, and Networked Publics* (New York: Peter Lang).

Sabbagh, D. (2011) 'Times Paywall Hits 100,000 But Pace of Growth Slows', guardian.co.uk, 30 June. Available at http://www.guardian.co.uk/media/2011/jun/30/thetimes-sundaytimes.

Salwen, M. B., B. Garrison and P. D. Driscoll (eds) (2005) *Online News and the Public* (Mahwah, NJ: Lawrence Erlbaum).

Sarikakis, K. and D. K. Thussu (eds) (2006) *Ideologies of the Internet* (Cresskill, NJ: Hampton Press)

Sawhney, H. (2010) 'The Cable Fables: The Innovative Imperative of Excess Capacity', in W. R. Neuman (ed.), *Media, Technology and Society: Theories of Media Evolution* (Ann Arbor: University of Michigan Press).

Schatz, R., S. Wagner, S. Egger and N. Jordan (2007) 'Mobile TV Becomes Social – Integrating Content with Communications', paper presented at the Proceedings of the ITI 2007 Conference, Croatia, 25–28 June.

Scholz, T. (2008) 'Market Ideology and the Myths of Web 2.0', *First Monday* vol. 13 no. 3. Available at http://www.uic.edu/htbin/cgiwrap/bin/ojs/index.php/fm/article/view/2138/1945.

Schudson, M. (2008) *Why Democracies Need an Unlovable Press* (Cambridge and Malden, MA: Polity Press).

Schudson, M. (2009) 'The New Media in the 2008 U.S. Presidential Campaign: The *New York Times* Watches Its Back', *Javnost-the Public* vol. 16, pp. 5–18.

Schudson, M. (2010) 'Political Observatories, Databases and News in the Emerging Ecology of Public Information', *Dædalus* vol. 139, pp. 100–9.

Schumpeter, J. A. (1943) *Capitalism, Socialism and Democracy* (London: George Allen & Unwin).

Scott, B. (2005) 'A Contemporary History of Digital Journalism', *Television and New Media* vol. 6, pp. 89–126.

Scott, D. (1963) 'First Home TV Tape', *Popular Science*, October, vols 94–6, pp. 208–9.

Seijdel, J. (ed.) (2007) *The Rise of the Informal Media: How Search Engines, Weblogs and You-Tube Change Public Opinion*, Open 13 (Rotterdam: NAI).

Seiter, E. (1999) *Television and New Media Audiences* (Oxford and New York: Clarendon Press).

Sennett, R. (1998) *The Corrosion of Character: The Personal Consequences of Work in the New Capitalism* (New York: Norton).

Sennett, R. (2006) *The Culture of the New Capitalism* (New Haven, CT: Yale University Press).

Sennett, R. (2008) *The Craftsman* (New Haven, CT: Yale University Press).

Setzer, F. and J. Levy (1991) *Broadcast Television in a Multichannel Marketplace* (Springfield, VA: US Dept of Commerce, National Technical Information Service).

Shiller, R. J. (2005) *Irrational Exuberance* (Princeton, NJ: Princeton University Press).

Siddique, H. (2010) 'Press Freedom Group Joins Condemnation of WikiLeaks' War Logs', Guardian.co.uk, 13 August. Available at http://www.guardian.co.uk/media/2010/aug/13/wikileaks-reporters-without-borders.

Siegel, L. (2007) *Against the Machine: Being Human in the Age of the Electronic Mob* (New York: Spiegel & Grau).

Silverstone, R. and L. Haddon (1996) 'Design and Domestication of Information and Communication Technologies: Technical Change and Everyday Life', in R. Mansell and R. Silverstone (eds), *Communication by Design: The Politics of Information and Communication Technologies* (Oxford: Oxford University Press), pp. 44–74.

Silverstone, R., E. Hirsch and D. Morley (eds) (1992) *Consuming Technologies: Media and Information in Domestic Spaces* (London: Routledge).

Simpson, J. A. (1999) *When a Word Is Worth a Thousand Pictures: Improved Television Access for Blind Viewers in the Digital Era* (Melbourne: Blind Citizens Australia).

Sinclair, J. (1999) *Latin American Television: A Global View* (Oxford and New York: Oxford University Press).

Sinclair, J., E. Jacka and S. Cunningham (eds) (1995) *New Patterns in Global Television: Peripheral Vision* (New York and London: Oxford University Press).

Skype (2010) 'Skype Files Registration Statement for Initial Public Offering', 8 August. Available at http://about.skype.com/press/2010/08/ipo.html.

Slack, J. D. and J. M. Wise (2005) *Culture + Technology: A Primer* (New York: Peter Lang).

Smith, J. (2010) *Spoken Word: Postwar American Phonograph Cultures* (Berkeley: University of California Press).

Srebeny, A. and G. Khiabany (2010) *Blogistan: The Internet and Politics in Iran* (London: I. B. Tauris).

Stafford, R. H. (1980) *Digital Television: Bandwidth Reduction and Communication Aspects* (New York: Wiley).

Starks, M. (2007) *Switching to Digital Television: UK Public Policy and the Market* (Bristol: Intellect).

Sterne, J. (2006) 'The MP3 as Cultural Artifact', *New Media & Society* vol. 8, pp. 825–42.

Sterne, J. (2007) 'Out with the Trash: On the Future of New Media', in C. R. Acland (ed.), *Residual Media* (Minneapolis and London: University of Minnesota Press), pp. 16–31.

Sterne, J. (2012) *MP3: The Meaning of a Format* (Durham, NC: Duke University Press).

Sun, W. (2002) *Leaving China: Media, Migration, and Transnational Imagination* (Lanham, MD: Rowman & Littlefield).

Tambini, D. and J. Cowling (2004) *From Public Service Broadcasting to Public Service Communications* (London: Institute for Public Policy Research).

Terrington, S. and C. Dollar (2005) 'Measuring the Value Created by the BBC', in D. Helm (ed.), *Can the Market Deliver?: Funding Public Service Television in the Digital Age* (London: John Libbey), pp. 60–77.

Thompson, E. P. (1963) *The Making of the English Working Class* (London: Victor Gollancz).

Thomson Reuters (2011) 'The Trust Principles'. Available at http://thomson reuters.com/about/trust_principles/.

Toffler, A. (1970) *Future Shock* (New York: Random House).

Toffler, A. (1980) *The Third Wave* (New York: Morrow).

Tracey, M. (1998) *The Decline and Fall of Public Sector Broadcasting* (Oxford and New York: Oxford University Press).

Tremayne, M. (ed.) (2007) *Blogging, Citizenship, and the Future of Media* (London: Routledge).

Trexler, K. (2007) 'The Edsel Show'. Available at http://www.ev1.pair.com/edsel/edselshow1.html.

Tuchman, J. (2010) 'Twitter Feeds and Blogs Tell Hidden Story of Mexico's Drug Wars', *Guardian.co.uk*, 26 September. Available at http://www.guardian.co.uk/world/2010/sep/26/twitter-blog-mexico-drug-wars.

Tunstall, J. (1996) *Newspaper Power: The New National Press in Britain* (Oxford and New York: Oxford University Press).

Turkle, S. (1995) *Life on the Screen: Identity in the Age of the Internet* (New York: Simon & Schuster).

Turner, F. (2006) *From Counterculture to Cyberculture: Stewart Brand, The Whole Earth Network, and the Rise of Digital Utopianism* (Chicago, IL: University of Chicago Press).

Turner, G. (2010) *Ordinary People and the Media: The Demotic Turn* (Los Angeles, CA: Sage).

Turner, G. and J. Tay (ed.) (2009) *Television Studies after TV: Understanding Television in the Post-Broadcast Era* (London and New York: Routledge).

Turner, G. and J. Tay (2010) 'Not the Apocalypse: Television Futures in the Digital Age', *International Journal of Digital Television* vol. 1, pp. 31–50.

Twitter (2011) 'Twitter 101: How Should I Get Started Using Twitter?'. Available at https://support.twitter.com/groups/31-twitter-basics/topics/104-welcome-to-twitter-support/articles/215585-twitter-101-how-should-i-get-started-using-twitter.

US House of Representatives (1984) *Developing Technologies for Television Captioning: Benefits for the Hearing Impaired*, Hearing before the Subcommittee on Science, Research, and Technology of the Committee on Science and Technology (Washington, DC: GPO).

Van Tassel, J. M. (2001) *Digital TV over Broadband: Harvesting Bandwidth* (Boston, MA: Focal Press).

Veljanovski, C. G. and W. D. Bishop (1983) *Choice by Cable: The Economics of a New Era in Television* (London: Institute of Economic Affairs).

Vink, N. (1998) *The Telenovela and Emancipation: A Study on Television and Social Change in Brazil* (Amsterdam: Royal Tropical Institute).

Visser, G. (2009) 'WikiLeaks Opens Leaked Documents', 26 November. Available at http://www.smartmobs.com/2009/11/26/wikileaks-opens-leaked-documents.

Vissol, T. (2006) *Is There a Case for an EU Information Television Station?* (Luxembourg: Office for Official Publications of the European Communities).

Von Hippel, E. (2005) *Democratizing Innovation* (Cambridge, MA: MIT Press).

Wahl-Jorgensen, K. (2010) 'News Production, Ethnography, and Power: On the Challenges to Newsroom-Centricity', in S. E. Bird (ed.), *The Anthropology of News and Journalism: Global Perspectives* (Bloomington: Indiana University Press), pp. 21–34.

Wasko, J. (1995) *Hollywood in the Information Age: Beyond the Silver Screen* (Austin: University of Texas Press).

Waterman, D. (2004) 'Business Models and Program Content', in E. Noam, J. Groebel and D. Gerbarg (eds), *Internet Television* (Mahwah, NJ: Lawrence Erlbaum), pp. 61–80.

Waterman, D. and A. Weiss (1997) *Vertical Integration in Cable Television* (Cambridge, MA: MIT Press; Washington, DC: AEI Press).

Wei, S. (2010) *Going Live in a Convergent Broadcasting Newsroom – A Case Study of Al Jazeera English,* MA thesis, University of Canterbury.

Wellman, B. and C. A. Haythornwaite (eds) (2002) *The Internet in Everyday Life* (Oxford: Blackwell).

Wikinews (2010) 'Wikinews: Mission Statement', 4 November. Available at http://en.wikinews.org/wiki/Wikinews:Mission_statement.

Williams, R. and D. Edge (1996) 'What Is the Social Shaping of Technology?', *Research Policy* vol. 25, pp. 856–99.

Winner, L. (1986) *The Whale and the Reactor: A Search for Limits in an Age of High Technology* (Chicago, IL: University of Chicago Press).

Winsbury, R. (1979) *The Electronic Bookstall: Push-Button Publishing on Videotex* (London: International Institute of Communications).

Winsbury, R. (ed.) (1981) *Viewdata in Action: A Comparative Study of Prestel* (London and New York: McGraw-Hill).

Woo, W. F. (2000) 'Public Journalism: A Critique', in A. J. Eksterowicz and R. N. Roberts (eds), *Public Journalism and Political Knowledge* (Lanham, MD: Rowman & Littlefield), pp. 21–42.

Woolfe, R. (1980) *Videotex: The New Television/Telephone Information Services* (London and Philadelphia, PA: Heyden).

Young, C. W. (2009) 'OhmyNews: Citizen Journalism in South Korea', in S. Allan and E. Thorsen (eds), *Citizen Journalism: Global Perspectives* (New York: Peter Lang), pp. 145–52.

Yu, H. (2010) 'Beyond Gatekeeping: J-blogging in China', *Journalism: Theory, Practice and Criticism* vol. 12, pp. 379–93.

Zuchetti, A. (2006) *The Illegal Downloading of Television Content from the Internet: Causes, Impacts and Outcomes,* Honours thesis, Department of Media and Communications, University of Sydney.

Index